WHO PUT LEMONS IN MY FRUIT OF THE SPIRIT?

Who Put Lemons in My Fruit of the Spirit?

Fresh-Squeezed Insights From the Book of Galatians

MARTHA BOLTON

SERVANT PUBLICATIONS
ANN ARBOR, MICHIGAN

Vine Books is an imprint of Servant Publications especially designed to serve evangelical Christians.

Servant Publications—Mission Statement

We are dedicated to publishing books that spread the gospel of Jesus Christ, help Christians to live in accordance with that gospel, promote renewal in the church, and bear witness to Christian unity.

Unless otherwise indicated all Scripture quotations are from the Holy Bible, New International Version, copyright 1973, 1978, 1984 by International Bible Society. Used by permission of Zondervan Publishing House. All rights reserved.

Published by Servant Publications
P.O. Box 8617
Ann Arbor, Michigan 48107
www.servantpub.com

Cover design: Paz Design Group, Salem, Oreg.

03 04 05 06 10 9 8 7 6 5 4 3 2 1

Printed in the United States of America
ISBN 1-56955-299-1

Library of Congress Cataloging-in-Publication Data

Bolton, Martha, 1951-

Library of Congress Cataloging-in-Publication Data

Bolton, Martha, 1951-
  Who put lemons in my fruit of the Spirit? : fresh-squeezed insights
from the book of Galatians / Martha Bolton.
     p. cm.
  ISBN 1-56955-299-1 (alk. paper)
  1. Youth–Religious life. 2. Youth–Conduct of life. 3. Bible. N.T.
Galatians–Criticism, interpretation, etc. I. Title.
  BV4850.B6365 2003
  242'.63–dc21

                                                            2003000247

Contents

U R 2 GOOD 2 B 4-GOTTEN

I recently came across my junior high school yearbook. It was fun to look back and read the different messages from friends and teachers. Touching sentiments like:

"You're a nut! Give my ears a break in History just once! ... Just kidding. Hope we'll always be friends."—Linda

"Martha, I really had a blast in Typing this semester. You're so funny. I want to wish you all the luck in the world now and especially when you're in high school."—Chris

And here's one I even wrote to myself ...

"Hi, Martha. This is Martha. It's been a pleasure having you around this semester. Hope to see you next year. I wish you all the luck and happiness throughout the years to come. Keep laughing! Your best friend and mine ... Martha"

I guess I had an empty page to fill up.

Greetings, well wishes, salutations—that's how people encourage one another. It's also how the writers of the Bible encouraged the people of their time.

Paul, who wrote the book of Galatians, begins Galatians (his letter to the churches of Galatia) with a greeting: "Grace and peace to you from God our Father and the Lord Jesus Christ."

This was his salutation. His "Dear People of Galatia ..." He was writing them to greet them and to address the issue of legalism versus grace. You see, it had come to his attention that they were having problems in this area. They were forgetting their justification had come through faith and not through works. Paul wanted to remind them that the gospel is not about anything we can or should do. It's all about what Jesus has already done on the cross.

The book of Galatians is Paul's letter to these churches. And it's still relevant for us today.

Thoughts to Ponder

If God wrote a letter to you right now, what do you think he would want to say about what his Son Jesus has already done for you?

If you were to write a letter to God right now, what would you say?

Bumper Sticker for the Day
The Bible: "You've Got Mail" from God.

Scripture to Stand On

Paul, an apostle—sent not from men nor by man, but by Jesus Christ and God the Father, who raised him from the dead, and all the brothers with me, to the churches in Galatia: "Grace and peace to you from God our Father and the Lord Jesus Christ."

GALATIANS 1:1-3

Hello Again, Lord ...

Lord, open up my mind as I study the book of Galatians and let me hear what you want to say to me about grace.

God's Will Will Do

Have you ever had your plans changed at the last minute? You were all ready to go somewhere, but then everything fell through. You went from your ideal Plan A to a less-than-perfect Plan B, and you weren't happy about it in the least!

So does this mean we should never make plans? No way! Can you imagine what the world would be like if that were the case?

"So when's the Christmas party?"

"I don't know. Just show up."

"When? Friday night?"

"Whenever."

"What time?"

"Surprise me."

"Who's coming?

"Beats me. But make sure you RSVP."

"Why?"

"So I'll know you're coming. You think I've made all these plans for nothing?"

Making plans is important. It's the mark of an achiever. It's how things get done and done right.

Yet sometimes while we're making our plans, we forget one very important thing—the "God Factor."

What's the God Factor?

It's realizing that God could have better plans than what you're planning for your day, year, or even your life.

After I wrote my first sample television script, I heard from the producer of the show that not only did he like it but he was going to call me in for a pitch session the following season. A pitch session is a chance for you to run some of your ideas by the producer; hopefully he will like one well enough to give you an assignment. When the show was cancelled the following season, however, my Plan A came to a screeching halt.

Yet God's Plan A started picking up speed. The gentleman who happened to be the creative consultant on the show, and who had taken my work to the producer in the first place, liked my work enough to recommend me to the comedy legend Bob Hope. I tried out for Bob and soon became his first woman staff writer.

We may not want to see it at the moment, but our Plan A usually pales next to God's Plan A.

Thoughts to Ponder

Have you ever had a time when your plans didn't work out, but you later discovered that God's plans were better?

Why do you think you're better off following God's plans?

Bumper Sticker for the Day
Make your plans in pencil. Let God write his in ink.

Scripture to Stand On

Now you, brothers, like Isaac, are children of promise.

GALATIANS 4:28

Hello Again, Lord ...

Lord, I know you have the best plans for my life. Don't let me miss them.

Hold It!

Mind holding my sweater?"

"Not at all."

"Here. Hold my soda."

"Sure thing."

"Carry my books for me."

"OK."

"This tuba's a pain. Can you carry it for a while?"

"Of course."

"Hey, what's happened to you? You're not any fun anymore. You never smile, you never laugh. I've got to find someone else to hang around with. You're really dragging me down."

Ever wonder what happened to your joy? Maybe you've lost it because you're carrying too many things for other people— things that they should be carrying for themselves. No, I'm not talking about sweaters, drinks, books, or tubas. Those can get heavy, too, but what I'm talking about is their problems.

"Can you cover for me Friday night? My boyfriend and I aren't getting along right now and we need to talk. And you know how my parents are. They won't let me go out with him anymore. So can I tell them I'm going to be with you?"

Or ...

"You've got to let me copy your homework. If I fail this class, I won't graduate."

And so on ... and so on ... and so on.

It's good to listen to your friends' problems, even offer advice, encouragement, and prayer. But you can't carry their problems for them. More importantly, God doesn't expect you to.

Making our own decisions and accepting responsibility for them is how we mature. You can try to help your friends make the right choices, but ultimately, it's their decision, and the consequences are theirs as well. If they make a wrong choice, you can and should be there for them, but not by doing something that God wouldn't want you to do. Rather, let them know that there are better choices they can make, and if they still end up making the wrong decision, then set your boundaries. Be a true friend to both yourself and to your friends. After all, life is going to give each of us our own set of problems to handle. If we try to step in and handle everyone else's problems for them, we're not going to have the strength to handle our own.

Thoughts to Ponder

Do you have a friend who has tried to get you to carry his or her problems? If so, how do you think you can help this friend improve his or her decision-making abilities?

In what ways do you think you can improve your ability to set boundaries?

Bumper Sticker for the Day
You can't soar like an eagle when you're a pack mule for everyone else.

Scripture to Stand On

... for each one should carry his own load.

GALATIANS 6:5

Hello Again, Lord ...

Lord, help me to remember that true friends have healthy boundaries.

Rising to the Occasion

I've never forgotten my high school cafeteria's cinnamon rolls. They were the best I've ever tasted. Cinnabon rolls are good, but they're not the same as my high school cinnamon rolls.

My husband came across a recipe for cinnamon rolls that looked close to those high school rolls, but when he made them, something went wrong. I think he went a little overboard on the yeast because each roll expanded to the size of a small tire. It was like a science fiction movie: "Run for your life! The rolls are coming!"

Yeast is an interesting ingredient. It works so well, most recipes call for only a little bit of it. Just a very small amount is all that's necessary to make cakes rise, rolls expand, or muffins peak up. The Bible even tells us that. You didn't know the Bible offered cooking tips, did you? It does. Right here in Galatians.

The point Paul is making with this cooking analogy is this—just as it takes only a little yeast to leaven a whole batch of dough, it doesn't take many good or bad actions to have an effect on the whole situation, either.

In other words, a little kindness goes a long way, a little encouragement, a little pointing out the positive, a little forgiveness, a little mercy, a little grace, a little love.

A little discouragement goes a long way, too. As does a little ridicule, a little meanness, a little putting down, a little pointing out the negative, a little bitterness, and a little unforgiveness.

You want a flat cake? Muffins that just sit there? Then by all means, skip the leavening. But if you want to bake like Sara Lee, you'd better use a little yeast.

Want to have a positive effect on someone's life? Try a pinch of grace, add a dash of mercy, and while you're at it, knead in a little forgiveness and love, too.

Thoughts to Ponder

Have you ever had someone add some mercy or encouragement to your life?

Did a little bit go a long way?

Bumper Sticker for the Day
Your little + God's much = all you need.

Scripture to Stand On

A little yeast works through the whole batch of dough.

GALATIANS 5:9

Hello Again, Lord ...

Lord, help me to never forget the power that is in a small amount of good.

The Perfect Club

It's clear that none of us living today are perfect. But what about all the perfect people in the Bible? Let's take David. He was called a man after God's own heart. That sounds pretty perfect to me. He was even chosen by God to be king after Saul's reign. You can't get much more perfect than that, right?

But wait a minute. Wasn't he the guy who saw a married woman bathing, had an affair with her, impregnated her, then had her husband killed? That can't be the same David, can it?

Oops. Same guy.

OK, so David wasn't perfect. But what about Moses? He was handpicked to lead God's people out of their enslavement in Egypt. That's a pretty big assignment. God wouldn't give something that important to just anybody. God even performed miracles for him, like parting the Red Sea. You'd have to be pretty high up on the Perfect Chart for God to do those kinds of miracles for you, right?

Uh ... didn't Moses kill a man?

Oops again. Guess we forgot about that little incident. Next ...

Well, there's Paul. He was always perfect, wasn't he? Nope. He used to persecute the church, remember?

OK, Peter. Wait, didn't he deny Jesus three times?

Jonah? Not him, either. Just ask the whale how perfect he was. Jonah's running from God gave the whale a major bellyache.

Go through the Bible and you'll find good people, righteous men and women of God, but you won't find a single perfect person, except Jesus.

Ever since the fall of Adam and Eve, God has had to use

imperfect people. Flawed people. Frightened people. Why? Because that's all he's had to work with. Outside of Jesus, none of us make the cut. Not without grace.

So if you're holding back from doing what God wants you to do because of feelings of inferiority, if your past mistakes and insecurities are keeping you from following God's call on your life, remember that you're in good company. No one has ever felt 100 percent qualified to do what God has called him or her to do.

Think about it—if God used only perfect people, every church would be silent, every religious bookstore would be empty, and every gospel concert would be a "no show." No one could be used by him.

God wants to make something out of your life. He wants to accomplish some pretty amazing things through you. So what's he waiting for? Is he waiting for you to present to him a perfect you? No, he's just waiting for a willing you.

Thoughts to Ponder

What do you think God is telling you when he discloses the imperfections of the people he chose to use?

Make a list of all those whom you believe are not included in the Scripture, "For all have sinned and fall short of the glory of God" (Romans 3:23).

Bumper Sticker for the Day
God's army is full of imperfect soldiers, and they win.

Scripture to Stand On

But the Scripture declares that the whole world is a prisoner of sin, so that what was promised, being given through faith in Jesus Christ, might be given to those who believe.

GALATIANS 3:22

Hello Again, Lord ...

Thank you, Lord, for making our imperfections perfect.

Who, Me?

What if Moses had stayed home instead of going before Pharoah? We know he hated public speaking. What if he had told God, "No way. You're not getting me up there in front of Pharoah. I can't do it! Find someone else!"

What if David had told God, "Did you see the size of that giant? I know you'll go with me, Lord, but *did you see the size of the giant?* Let's talk reality here. He is twice my size! I can't take him on. I'm just a kid!"

What if Noah had told God, "Build an ark? Do you have any idea how much work you're asking me to do? Besides, the neighbors already look at me funny. Why give them something else to talk about?"

What if every single person who ever did anything great for the Lord was too small or too shy or too tired or too insecure or too busy or too whatever? It's easy to list your shortcomings and use them for an excuse as to why you can't do this or that for God. We all have things we have to overcome. Even the people in the Bible had things to overcome. Yet the ones who accomplished the most for God didn't let their shortcomings become their excuses.

Moses wasn't a good orator, but he went and spoke to Pharoah anyway, along with his brother Aaron. David was only a young boy, but he stood up to Goliath anyway. Noah probably didn't have the energy to work on an ark day after day, week after week, year after year, but he did it anyway.

What excuses are you using for not doing what God wants you to do?

Thoughts to Ponder

How does it make you feel to know that some of the greatest men and women of God felt unqualified to do what God wanted them to do?

Why do you think God would rather use someone who is obedient than someone who is more qualified?

Bumper Sticker for the Day
When God asks, just do it!

Scripture to Stand On

But when God, who set me apart from birth and called me by his grace, was pleased to reveal his Son in me so that I might preach him among the Gentiles, I did not consult any man, nor did I go up to Jerusalem to see those who were apostles before I was, but I went immediately into Arabia and later returned to Damascus.

GALATIANS 1:15-17

Hello Again, Lord ...

I know the things that I can't do. Help me to believe, Lord, in what I can do through you.

Trading Spaces

There is a very popular show on television right now called "Trading Spaces." The premise of the show is for neighbors to exchange homes for one day and redecorate one room of each other's house. Most of the time each couple, along with an assigned designer, will capture the style and taste of the homeowner. Sometimes they don't.

It's not easy to get into the mind of someone else, to know that person's likes and dislikes. You probably already realize that every Christmas when you go shopping for that perfect gift for your loved ones. You buy things you hope they'll like, or if they've given you a Christmas list, you might buy what they've written on it.

Yet, Christmas shopping for your loved ones or redesigning a neighbor's house is a piece of cake compared to trying to get into the mind of a total stranger. When you're dealing with someone you know, at least you have some idea, however vague, of that person's favorite colors, general style, and so on. However, when you don't know the first thing about someone, how in the world can you decide what he or she would like? You're at a tremendous disadvantage.

Judging people without fully knowing their circumstances or understanding their hearts is equally presumptuous. You may be able to see the situation on the surface, but to understand what makes people act the way they do, say the things they say, and feel the way they feel takes a little more information.

Yet we usually don't have that kind of information. We don't always have it for those who are close to us, much less for complete strangers. Only they and God are privy to that information. That's why he told us to leave the judging to him. He knows everything there is to know about the situation and the people involved. He knows their history, their dreams, and their fears, and he has heard all the prayers that they've prayed in secret. He is the one who's best qualified to judge their actions, because only he knows the whole story.

"Trading Spaces" is a popular show. Yet until we can truly trade spaces with the person we're judging, our judging will always be a little skewed. God's judgments aren't. They're always right, they're always fair, and they always have the person's best interest in mind.

Thoughts to Ponder

Think of someone who is the topic of "discussion" in your circle of friends, your family, or at your church. Would you say that there might be more to the story than any of you realizes?

Who would you rather have judge you? God, or someone who knows nothing about you?

Bumper Sticker for the Day
Walk a mile in someone's shoes and you'll soon want your own back.

Scripture to Stand On

Clearly no one is justified before God by the law ...

GALATIANS 3:11a

Hello Again, Lord ...

Thank you, Lord, for being a fair and loving judge.

Plant Life

My son has a garden in our backyard. This year he planted tomatoes, cucumbers, cauliflower, cabbage, radishes, spinach, eggplant, and peas. He waters it every evening and pulls any weeds that might have started to grow in it.

The other day while I was at the grocery store, I bought a watermelon that looked almost like a giant cucumber. It was oblong, was sort of a striped green.

Before I got it home, a funny thought hit me. I could sneak into the backyard and lay the watermelon down on the ground by the cucumber plants. Then, when it came time for my son to water his plants, he would think that a record-breaking cucumber had grown overnight in his garden!

I was already laughing when I pulled up to the house. Seeing that my son hadn't watered yet, I took the watermelon out of the car and walked around the house to the backyard. I strategically placed the watermelon under the cucumber vines, then walked back around to the front door and entered the house.

"How's your garden doing?" I asked after putting the rest of the groceries away.

"Thanks for reminding me," he said, making his way toward the back door. "I need to go water."

The rest of the family stood at the back window, watching as he walked toward his garden. He stopped, did a double take, then realizing it was a watermelon, had a good laugh.

The laws of nature are pretty certain. If you plant cucumbers, you're not going to get watermelons. Green beans won't grow from a tomato plant, and cauliflower won't grow from cabbage plants. Whatever you plant, that's what you're going to harvest. It's as simple as that.

Paul tells us here in Galatians that whatever we plant in life, that's what we're going to harvest, too. If we plant good things, we'll reap good things. If we plant love, we'll reap love. If we plant understanding, we'll reap understanding. If we plant peace, we'll reap peace.

By the same token, if we plant jealousy, we'll reap jealousy. If we plant unforgiveness, we'll reap unforgiveness. If we plant hatred, we'll reap hatred. What we plant is what is going to grow. It's as simple as that.

Thoughts to Ponder

What kind of seeds do you think you are sowing in life?

Can you think of an instance when you hoped to get a different result from what you had "planted"? What did you learn from that experience?

Bumper Sticker for the Day
There are no surprises in life's garden.

Scripture to Stand On

Do not be deceived: God cannot be mocked. A man reaps what he sows.
GALATIANS 6:7

Hello Again, Lord ...

Lord, help me to plant only what I want to see grow.

A Deaf Ear

I knew a girl once who took pride in her reputation for never saying anything bad about anyone. Many people admired that about her. The only problem was that she listened to plenty of it. Listening to and not stopping gossip is almost as bad as gossiping.

Why? Well, ask yourself this—if one of your best friends was in a conversation where your name was brought up, would you want her to sit and listen or would you want her to stick up for you? Of course you'd want her to stick up for you. By merely listening and not correcting any misinformation, she implies that she agrees with the gossipers. That's not the kind of friend I would want, I'm sure it's not the kind of friend you would want, and it's definitely not the kind of friend God wants us to be.

The next time you're caught in the company of a gossiper, here's what to do:

If you hear lies, counter them with truth.

If you hear innuendo, counter it with fact.

If you hear suspicion, counter it with trust.

If you hear slander, counter it with defense.

If you hear negative, counter it with positive.

If you hear misquotes, counter them with corrections.

If you hear a cry for justice, counter it with a call for grace.

If you hear accusations, counter them with forgiveness.

If you hear character assassination, counter it with character validation.

Maybe the real problem with gossip isn't so much that so many people do it, but that so few do anything to stop it.

Thoughts to Ponder

Do you agree that it's just as wrong to listen to gossip as it is to spread it?

What do you think would happen if we all started meeting gossip with some of the preceding suggestions?

Bumper Sticker for the Day
Sometimes our conversations need a content rating.

Scripture to Stand On

If you keep on biting and devouring each other, watch out or you will be destroyed by each other.

GALATIANS 5:15

Hello Again, Lord ...

Lord, help me to remember that when it comes to gossip, we should all have a hearing problem.

Holy Circles

I t's a good thing God doesn't get tired. Or dizzy. Because from the way so many people claim to speak for him, it sounds as if he does a lot of flip-flopping between sides.

This person says God is a Democrat. That one says he's a Republican.

This one says he's a God of love, so do whatever you want. That one says he's a God of judgment and you can't do anything fun, least of all laugh or have any joy in your life.

And can't you just imagine what God's date book would look like if he went according to everyone else's schedule for him? There have been so many false predictions for Christ's return and the end times, there would be dates crossed out all over the place.

1984. The end of the world.

Not even close.

January 1, 2000—Y2K. The end of the world.

Nope.

Let's try January 1, 2001. That's the real millennium anyway.

Oops. Wrong again.

People have even boxed God into deadlines for when he's going to answer their prayers.

"My answer is going to come by Wednesday. God told me."

And when it doesn't ...

"I must have misunderstood him. It sounded like Wednesday, but he probably said Friday."

Friday comes and again nothing happens. So they continue giving God "extensions," cutting him slack, and making their adjustments to his seemingly "ever-changing" schedule.

Yet God's schedule hasn't changed. He just doesn't want to work on our timelines. He has his own calendar, and nothing needs to be crossed out or changed. His timing is always perfect.

Some people even think God must like to flip-flop about his choice for our lifetime mate. Why else would the same celebrity receive letters from a handful of different people saying that God "told them that they were to marry" that celebrity? Yet, think about it—God isn't going to tell six different guys that he wants them to marry the same girl, or tell six different girls that they're to marry the same guy. If he did that, he'd be breaking his own laws, and God doesn't break his laws. So obviously someone's listening to his or her own desires, rather than to God's.

God isn't wishy-washy. He doesn't take one side, then switch over to the other side when it's more convenient. He doesn't tell numerous people to marry the same person. He hasn't postponed the date of his Son's return. It's the same date it's always been. It hasn't changed, and he's still the only one who knows what it is.

That's why, when it comes to speaking for God, we need to stick to what the Bible tells us he says and thinks. That's something we don't have to guess about.

Thoughts to Ponder

Why do you think it's important to know God's character and his words for yourself?

Do you feel you spend enough time reading God's Word?

Bumper Sticker for the Day
God's words bring peace, not panic; direction, not confusion.

Scripture to Stand On

I assure you before God that what I am writing you is no lie.

GALATIANS 1:20

Hello Again, Lord ...

Lord, help me to know your character and your words so well that I'll never mistake someone else's agenda for your calendar.

Good Intentions

What do you do when people ask you to pray for them? Do you have every good intention, but then forget all about it and go about your day? Do you tell yourself that others will be praying, so you don't need to worry about it? Or do you actually take the time to stop and pray?

When people ask us to pray for a specific need in their life, they're depending on us to do just that. They're not saying it to start a conversation. They're asking us to pray. They're counting on us to pray.

Just imagine if someone asked you for a ride to the doctor. It wouldn't do that person much good if you never showed up, would it? It's the same with a prayer request. Promises of prayer don't do any good either. Your prayer has to show up in heaven.

It's not that you don't mean well. You add it to your list of things to do, but then get busy and never seem to get around to it. Or you honestly forget. You fully intend to pray for that person's need, but it just slips your mind.

How would you feel if someone came up to you and said, "How's your aunt doing? I've been meaning to pray for her ever since you asked me to, but, well, I'm just so absent-minded these days. Hope she's doing better."

Then you have to tell them that Aunt Thelma never recovered.

It may have been God's will for Aunt Thelma to go on

home to heaven, but hearing that someone forgot to pray for her isn't going to be very comforting, is it?

You need to treat other people's needs with the same urgency with which you'd like your needs to be treated. Not only should you assure people that you'll pray; you also need to do it.

Thoughts to Ponder

When someone asks you to pray for a need, do you tend to follow through with your promise or do you get sidetracked and forget all about it?

When you have a need, how do you want people to handle your requests for prayer?

Bumper Sticker for the Day
Unprayed prayers = Unanswered prayers.

Scripture to Stand On

The entire law is summed up in a single command: "Love your neighbor as yourself."

GALATIANS 5:14

Hello Again, Lord ...

Lord, you know all the things I need to pray about. Help me to remember them, too.

How Much?

Pop Quiz.

Now before you start moaning, let me assure you that I won't show up at your house to collect your paper and grade it. This test is for your eyes only.

Write down your answers to the following questions:

To earn God's love, it would require:

_____ meals served to the homeless.

_____ visits to a convalescent home.

no more than _____ church services missed.

no more than _____ missed opportunities to share your faith.

serving on at least _____ youth committees.

singing in the choir for at least _____ years.

never committing the following "major" sins:

_____

_____

_____

being at least better than the following people:

_____

_____

Even if you didn't actually fill in the blanks, I hope you did think about your answers. It's interesting to analyze what it is that we think we have to do to earn God's love.

The book of Galatians talks a lot about legalism. It corrects some misconceptions of what the gospel is all about. You see, none of us are or ever will be good enough to earn God's love. That includes our pastors, our families, our friends, and everyone else in our lives. Only Christ was perfect. That's why we all need grace. We can't measure up on our own. Because of that fact, we wouldn't want to stand before a perfect God and be judged on our own goodness. We have to stand before God in grace.

So you can forget all about measuring up to someone else or trying to do this or that to earn God's love. You already have it. His love was a gift to you. A gift you couldn't earn and don't have to earn. A gift you didn't deserve, and no one can take it away.

What do you have to do to earn God's love?

Accept it.

Thoughts to Ponder

Are you surprised at the things you were thinking you had to do to earn God's love?

How does it make you feel to know that God's love isn't dependent upon your performance?

Bumper Sticker for the Day
What's the dress code for heaven? Grace.

Scripture to Stand On

You who are trying to be justified by law have been alienated from Christ; you have fallen away from grace.

GALATIANS 5:4

Hello Again, Lord ...

Thank you, Lord, for giving me what I could never earn—your love.

Predictable
Unpredictability

L ife is unpredictable. On January 17, 1994, residents of the San Fernando Valley in Southern California were awakened to the violent shaking of a major earthquake. I was one of those residents. It was not a fun way to wake up. Sixty-one people were killed and over 8,000 were injured. It was a holiday, Martin Luther King's birthday. Most people had planned on sleeping in that day, but something else was in store for us. There was no warning ahead of time. The quake just hit. The earth shook. Buildings fell. Fires erupted. People were injured. Some died, including the sister-in-law of a friend of ours, who died when a three-story apartment building in Northridge collapsed, literally burying the first floor.

Exactly one year later, another quake, measuring 7.2 on the Richter scale, struck Japan, killing 5,100 and injuring nearly 27,000 people. Again, there was no warning.

In 1974 there was a "Super Tornado Outbreak" that affected a span of thirteen states. The tornadoes killed 330 people. To date, it was the worst tornado outbreak in U.S. history. Those 330 people didn't know the week before that their lives were going to be over in only seven days.

Floods and mudslides hit Southern California in 1969, killing over 100 people, and the 1976 Loveland, Colorado, flood left 139 dead. There have been plenty of other floods before and since that have struck just as suddenly.

Hurricane Hugo claimed 71 lives in 1989 when it hit both South and North Carolina. In 1993, 47 people were killed when Amtrak's Sunset Limited, bound for Miami, jumped the rails on a weakened bridge and plunged into the Big Bayou Canot.

Now think about where you were when those terrorists were flying passenger-filled airliners into the World Trade Center in New York City. What were you thinking about just moments before? Did the possibility of something so horrible happening in our world even enter your mind? Of course not. It was the unthinkable, the unimaginable.

Life is unpredictable. We don't know from one minute to the next what could happen in our world, at our schools, or in our families. While we're busy preparing ourselves for the impending death of our grandmother, our cousin could be injured in a car accident and find himself hanging onto life. While we're stressing over our upcoming history test, our best friend could become seriously ill and everything about our life might change in an instant.

Does that mean we should walk around depressed or fearful, knowing that something awful could happen at any minute?

Absolutely not!

Why? Because we have a God who is in control of the world and everything that happens in it. Nothing catches him off guard. He has promised to be with us every minute of every day, through whatever life throws our way.

Life is unpredictable. God is constant.

Thoughts to Ponder

Have you ever had your well-thought-out plans disrupted in an instant?

Why do you think God allows life to be unpredictable?

Bumper Sticker for the Day
Blessed assurance is our blessed insurance.

Scripture to Stand On

But the fruit of the Spirit is ... peace.

GALATIANS 5:22

Hello Again, Lord ...

With all the uncertainties of this life, you, Lord, are the only place I can put my trust.

Keep Out!

Have you ever gone into self-protection mode? You figure that if you don't feel, you won't hurt, so you shut down and put up a wall around your emotions.

It works ... but only to a point.

None of us enjoy having our feelings trampled on, or being treated like a doormat. We don't like being gossiped about, lied about, or left out, especially if it happens over and over and over again. So a protective wall sounds like a good idea, doesn't it? After all, isn't that what the ancient cities used to do to protect themselves?

The problem is, though, that by walling out the mean-spirited, inconsiderate, and rude people in your life, you might also be walling out some pretty nice people. And you'll never know how much they might have loved you or do love you if you never lower your walls to let them in.

It's not easy, though. The minute you lower your walls, it seems the bullies come racing back in to start up right where they left off. Still, it's a risk worth taking. You might even find yourself getting a little bit stronger, more able to stand up for yourself, each time you lower those walls.

So if you've erected a few walls to protect yourself from certain people, remember that those same walls could be keeping out friends as well—new friends who might be hesitant to try to scale that wall, and old friends who probably had nothing to do with the wall being erected in the first place.

Bring down those walls, one brick at a time, let love in and learn how to set reasonable boundaries, and before long, you'll be able to handle whoever walks into your life.

Thoughts to Ponder

Have you built a protective wall against someone?

Do you think your wall might be causing you to miss out on other friendships?

Bumper Sticker for the Day
Walls are never a good fashion statement.

Scripture to Stand On

What has happened to all your joy?

GALATIANS 4:15a

Hello Again, Lord ...

Lord, help me to remember that I don't have to be a doormat, but I don't have to build a fortress around my emotions, either.

Sinking Fast

Have you ever been in a boat when the wind started to kick up? I was in one once, and it's no fun. We were returning home from Catalina to Los Angeles, and the boat we were in hit every wave with the gentleness of a sumo wrestler. We were tossed to the right and tossed to the left. The only way we weren't tossed was upside down, and we even came close to that a few times. It wasn't, as the brochure said, "the best time of our lives."

Instead of the sales pitch, the brochure should have given us the following top ten warning signs ...

Ten Signs That Your Ship Is in Trouble

The Coast Guard just picked you up on their radar screen as a submarine.

You just saw a dolphin floating by on a deck chair.

You crawl into bed and get tangled up in seaweed.

You don't remember the cruise ship having that third swimming pool before.

Bubbles are coming out of your mouth every time you talk.

The only graffiti written on the ship is "S.O.S."

All the other passengers are wearing scuba gear.

Sharks have lined up to spell out the word, "Buffet!"

The shuffleboard court is vertical.

The ship rats are lowering the life rafts and paddling away.

If you see any of these signs, it might be time to bring on the Coast Guard!

Do you know that God is our rescuer in life? When we are buffeted by the winds of trouble, discouragement, hurt, loss, or whatever else is tossing us this way or that way, we can take comfort in knowing that he has the power to calm the storm. If he doesn't choose to, though, he also has the power to see us through it.

Either way, we're in good hands.

Thoughts to Ponder

Does it feel like you're being tossed in the winds of life right now?

Why do you think it's important to stay close to God in times like these?

Bumper Sticker for the Day
In the middle of the storm, don't climb out of the lifeboat.

Scripture to Stand On

... who gave himself for our sins to rescue us from the present evil age, according to the will of our God and Father.

GALATIANS 1:4

Hello Again, Lord ...

Lord, when it feels like I'm sinking, remind me that you're my lifeboat.

Hidden Truth

What if someone developed a truth pill that made us tell the truth in all situations? It could make life pretty interesting, couldn't it?

"My heart goes out to you," we'd start to say when someone we didn't really care for told us of some struggle. Yet as soon as we started to talk, the words would change to, "Well, it's about time God answered my prayer and gave you what you deserve!"

What if when we started to promise to keep a friend's confidence, the truth came bubbling out of our mouths instead in the form of, "Hurry up and tell me so I can start making the phone calls."

If we could speak only the truth, how much of what we say would be changed?

"That new haircut is horrible. What were you thinking?"

"I don't have time to listen to your problems. Go tell someone who cares."

"I'm only saying 'hi' to you to make myself look good because everyone knows I go to church and all. But for goodness sakes, don't think you can hang around me and my friends at lunch."

Luckily for us, there is no truth pill, but don't you wonder why we play games like this in the first place? No one needs "friend impersonators." What good are people like that when we really need them?

If our hearts don't really go out to people in pain, if we take joy in their discomfort, *they're* not the problem. The problem is in our hearts. If we make phone calls to all of our friends after someone has confided something in us, then the confidential situation isn't the problem. The problem is our idea of friendship. Of course, if their safety is at risk and if that is truly our concern, then we should certainly discuss it with our parents, school principal, pastor, or some other trusted adult, but not the entire student body.

Truth. Real friendships are based on it.

Thoughts to Ponder

How closely does what you say resemble what's in your heart?

Do you want your friends to be honest with you about your relationship, or would you be OK with a friend who was only a friend to your face?

Bumper Sticker for the Day
Be the kind of friend you want for a friend.

Scripture to Stand On

But the fruit of the Spirit is ... faithfulness.

GALATIANS 5:22

Hello Again, Lord ...

Lord, give me true friends and help me to be a true friend myself.

Guest of Honor

When NBC hosted a birthday party for Bob Hope, as one of his writers, I was invited, along with my husband, to attend the festivities. On the night of the event, we drove to the NBC parking lot, parked our van, and got out.

As we walked toward the red-carpet entrance that was lined on both sides with paparazzi, the realization suddenly hit me that there had to be another place for the writers to enter. Surely, we weren't supposed to walk down the red carpet with the celebrities. The paparazzi would be trying to take a picture of some superstar and we'd be blocking the shot. No, there was another entrance for writers. I was sure of it.

So I started looking for it. I walked around the left side of the building until I found a couple of unmarked doors. They were locked. I walked down the right side of the building. Same story. *Where is the "writer's entrance"?* I wondered as I continued to search the sides of the building for a more suitable entrance.

I finally walked toward the bushes and, with my high heels sinking into the dirt with each step, I squeezed my way up to the door. The cameramen and the others who were standing along the red carpet must have thought I was trying to crash the party, because they wouldn't let me through.

Finally, my husband just took me aside and said, "Martha, what are you doing? We have an invitation. We're supposed to walk down the red carpet like everyone else."

He was right, of course. We had been invited by the guest of honor himself. We had every right to walk down the carpet in front of all the paparazzi and join the party.

So I quit trying to slip in unnoticed and walked toward the entrance like all the other invited guests. And you know what? No one stopped me. I went into the party and had a wonderful time.

I can't help but wonder how many times we lose out on what God has planned for us because of feelings of inadequacy or fear, or because we simply forget who it is that has invited us to the party. God himself has given us our invitation, but we're too busy trying to find a way that's more suitable for us, a way through the bushes and dirt. And we miss out on so much.

Thoughts to Ponder

Have you ever let your insecurities hold you back from something with which God might have wanted to bless you?

How does it make you feel to know that God has personally invited you to his eternal party?

Bumper Sticker for the Day
RSVP for eternity.

Scripture to Stand On

So you are no longer a slave, but a son; and since you are a son, God has made you also an heir.

GALATIANS 4:7

Hello Again, Lord ...

Lord, thank you for being our friend in high places.

What's Up With Everything That's Down?

Who gets you down? That boy at school? That girl at church? Someone in your family? Is there someone in your life who never seems to have anything good to say to you? No matter what you do, it's not enough. You don't measure up. It's like you have to meet some unspoken standard. He reminds you of your past. You take one step forward, she pushes you two steps backward. While you're pointing out how much you've changed, this person is pointing out how much further you have to go.

In his letter to the Galatians Paul was writing to caution the church of Galatia about this type of judgmentalness.

When Jesus confronted someone about his or her sin, Paul knew he did it with mercy. In fact, the ones Jesus was hardest on were the Pharisees, the legalistic people of his day.

Paul knew that:

Legalism demands perfection in us. Grace offers perfection in Christ.

Legalism limits mercy. Grace freely gives it.

Legalism points to the law. Grace points to the cross.

Legalism requires. Grace encourages.

Legalism condemns. Grace forgives.

Legalism reminds. Grace forgets.

Legalism puts down. Grace lifts up.
Legalism withholds love. Grace is love.

When Paul wrote to the churches of Galatia, he knew the damage that legalism could do and was already doing. He also knew the power of grace. He wanted the Galatians to walk in grace. He pleaded with them not to let legalism deter them. He wanted them to keep their eyes on what Jesus had done on the cross, instead of what they could ever do to earn that sacrifice. He knew that when Jesus said, "It is finished," it was finished.

Thoughts to Ponder

Why do you think Paul got so frustrated over legalism?

Have you encountered any legalistic attitudes? How does grace measure up against this attitude?

Bumper Sticker for the Day
Gifts don't come with a bill.

Scripture to Stand On

For if the inheritance depends on the law, then it no longer depends on a promise; but God in his grace gave it to Abraham through a promise.
GALATIANS 3:18

Hello Again, Lord ...

Lord, thank you that your grace is ... amazing.

Standing Up

Have you ever had to oppose someone to his or her face because that person was in the wrong? It's not easy, is it? Some people enjoy confrontation, maybe even live for it. Yet for those of us who shy away from conflict, it's a difficult situation under the best of circumstances. It's much easier to live your life ignoring other people's insensitive behaviors.

Once in a while, though, you may have to stand up for yourself. Or for someone else. That's what Paul felt he had to do here with Peter on the matter of legalism versus grace. Paul wanted to make sure that the gospel of grace was being preached, and he felt so strongly about it that he had to confront Peter over it.

Ideally, when you confront someone over something, he or she will listen. If your complaint has merit, the one you are confronting should see your point. If it doesn't, he or she should still hear you out, and you should then hear him or her out. If both parties maintain their separate opinions, that's all right, too. But you've done what you felt you needed to do.

Paul knew he needed to defend the concept of grace. He knew that the people were unnecessarily living under the condemnation of legalism. He wanted them to live under grace. He wanted them to appreciate the gift that God had given them through his Son. A gift that we've been given, too.

Thoughts to Ponder

Do you have a difficult time confronting others?

Why do you think the subject of grace was so important to Paul?

Bumper Sticker for the Day
To see eye-to-eye, sometimes you have to start face-to-face.

Scripture to Stand On

When Peter came to Antioch, I opposed him to his face, because he was clearly in the wrong.

GALATIANS 2:11

Hello Again, Lord ...

Lord, thank you for my voice. Help me to use it when I need to, while still giving it plenty of rest.

Wake-Up Calls

Most hotels and motels offer a service called "wake-up calls." This means that the on-site operator will call your room at whatever time you request, to wake you up. If you forget to bring your watch on your trip, this is a great service. When the curtains of a hotel or motel room are drawn, it's easy to oversleep. What might seem like seven o'clock in the morning could very well be two o'clock in the afternoon.

"This is your 7 A.M. wake-up call," the voice on the other end of the line will say. You mumble a thanks, hang up the phone, and now the choice is yours whether to go back to sleep or get out of bed. Either way, the hotel has done its part. You know what time it is. You've been alerted.

Do you know the Bible gives us wake-up calls, too? The Book of Galatians is full of them. It warns us about such things as immorality, hatred, jealousy, selfishness, troublemaking, and rage. It warns us against conceit. It warns us against becoming weary in well-doing. It tells us that we'll reap what we sow. It warns us against thinking we're something we're not. It tells us not to compare ourselves with others. It warns us against those who would discourage us. It warns us against those who would condemn us and try to nullify Christ's grace. It warns us against legalism. It warns us against false doctrines.

Wake-up calls. They can bring us out of a stupor of immoral behavior, apathy, discouragement, and feelings of worthlessness. They give us the option to get up and do something about the situation in which we find ourselves or to roll over and go back to sleep. Either way, God has done his part. He has given us the wake-up call. What we choose to do about it is now up to us.

Thoughts to Ponder

Do you feel that God has been trying to give you a wake-up call?

Why do you think it's important to pay attention to God's wake-up calls?

Bumper Sticker for the Day
Blinders are never part of a good soldier's uniform.

Scripture to Stand On

I fear for you, that somehow I have wasted my efforts on you.

GALATIANS 4:11

Hello Again, Lord ...

Lord, help me to wake up and pay attention every time you call.

Help! I'm Whining and I Can't Shut Up!

Have you spent much time around a complainer? I'm not talking about the type of people who have a bad day every once in a while. I'm talking about people who have a bad day every day. Every minute of every hour of every day. Nothing ever goes right for them. They're living at Calamity Central. Chicken Little would have seemed like an eternal optimist around one of these people. Their whole lives are one long string of complaints. If anything goes right, they're the last one to see it.

And of course, things do go right. Lots of good things happen to them throughout their day. The fact that they got up in the morning means at least one thing went right for them—they're alive and breathing and capable of at least crawling out of bed. The fact that there's a roof over their heads means something else went right—a meteor didn't hit their houses while they were sleeping. If their cars started and got them to work or school, or the bus showed up and didn't have a flat meant a few more things went right.

Even if they hate school, they have one to go to. And the fact that they have something to eat, even if it's tuna pancakes, means they don't have to go hungry. If they got dressed, that means they had clothes to put on. If all the hot water was gone by the time they took their shower, that means there was running water in their houses.

Plenty of things go right for each of us every single day. Yet some of us are so used to taking them for granted, we don't even see our blessings.

The next time you feel like making a negative comment, ask yourself what you might be able to appreciate about the situation instead. There's usually something there, you just have to keep looking until you find it.

Don't misunderstand—plenty of things do go wrong in life. Yet if we focus all of our attention on the calamities, if we're walking Disaster Depots, we miss out on all that can be celebrated ... and appreciated.

We can't control everything that happens in our lives, but we can control our reactions.

Whine—it doesn't get better with time.

Thoughts to Ponder

Would you say that you're most often a grateful person or a whiner?

Do you think God enjoys hearing our whining?

Bumper Sticker for the Day
Blessings—count them, and you can count on them.

Scripture to Stand On

So those who have faith are blessed along with Abraham, the man of faith.

GALATIANS 3:9

Hello Again, Lord ...

Lord, help me not to take up your time complaining when there are so many things for which I should be thanking you.

Future Home

According to a report on CNN, when Ed Headrick, inventor of the Frisbee, died in August 2002, his family had a unique request. They wanted to have his remains cremated and the ashes molded into several Frisbees. One Frisbee would be saved for archival purposes, and the others would be tossed among family and friends in memory of Ed. As heartfelt as I'm sure this final farewell was, it still must have made for an interesting funeral, don't you think?

Hopefully, you won't have to face your own mortality for many, many years to come. I pray that each of you will be given eighty or ninety, maybe even a hundred years to live. Yet there's no guarantee of that. None of us are guaranteed our next week, our next day, or even our next breath. Only God knows when our time on this earth will be up.

We can know, though, where we're going to go after leaving this world. We can have our reservation for eternity locked in. We don't have to question our final destination.

Before ascending to heaven, Jesus told his followers that he was going to prepare a place for them, a place in heaven. If you want to get a glimpse of this incredible place, read the Book of Revelation. It gives some pretty awesome descriptions of heaven.

So, whether your family plans a final farewell like Ed's or something a little more traditional, it really doesn't matter. The important thing is to live every minute of your life to the fullest, to accomplish those things that you were meant to accomplish for God, and to never lose sight of what's waiting for you on the other side.

Thoughts to Ponder

What do you think is the best thing about heaven?

List some ways that you can make the best use of your time here on earth.

Bumper Sticker for the Day
So many searching, so little time.

Scripture to Stand On

If you belong to Christ, then you are Abraham's seed, and heirs according to the promise.

GALATIANS 3:29

Hello Again, Lord ...

Thank you, Lord, for the promise of heaven.

Pointing Fingers

Many of us manage to find all the time in the world to inspect other people's lives, down to the most finite detail, but when it comes to judging our own behaviors, we have little energy or interest left.

"I've heard he has a drinking problem," she says, while illegally downloading music on her computer.

"I saw her cheating on the final," he says, while mailing off his college application with an exaggerated number of community service hours listed on it.

Do you think that's why God has told us to leave the judging to him? Maybe he knows that, if done correctly, our self-examinations will leave us little time to judge other people. He knows we have enough in our own lives to keep us busy. All we have to do is peek around the facade we show others and we'll see our imperfections are right there, shining bright and clear.

Self-examinations are the most accurate examinations anyway, because we're the only ones who know the whole story behind our motives, our histories, and our particular situations. We don't have all this information when passing judgment on others. We don't know all the facts. So we fill in the blanks, make up our own interpretations, speculate, exaggerate, and condemn.

God doesn't work like that. He has all the facts, from beginning to end. He sees the hearts of the people involved. He knows the history of the situation. He sees the faults of both the accused and the accuser. That's why he's always the best judge.

Thoughts to Ponder

Who would you say you spend the most time judging—yourself or other people?

Why do you think most of us don't spend enough time looking inward?

Bumper Sticker for the Day
**Grace ... the amount we pour on others is the amount
God will pour on us.**

Scripture to Stand On

Each one should test his own actions. Then he can take pride in himself, without comparing himself to somebody else.

GALATIANS 6:4

Hello Again, Lord ...

Lord, thank you for being a fair and merciful judge.

Never Say Never

I'd never talk to my brother that way," you say. Yet the next day you find yourself in the middle of the biggest fight you've ever had with him and you end up calling him every name you can think of.

"I can't believe I acted like that," you write in your apology note afterward. "I don't know what happened to me."

When we say we'd never do something, there often comes a test of that vow afterward. Maybe not that day, or the next day, or even the next year. Yet eventually, it'll come. That's why it's usually not a good idea to say never.

None of us can accurately predict how we will behave under varying circumstances. In the safe and secure Upper Room, Peter nobly told Jesus that he would never deny him. Yet after Jesus was arrested and the circumstances had changed, that vow was tested and Peter failed. Three times.

In other words, that commandment that we so piously vow to never break might be the first one we violate when our circumstances change.

"I'd never ..."

"I'd never ..."

"I'd never ..."

It doesn't matter what word we use to finish those sentences, the fact of the matter is that we don't know what we'll do in different circumstances. We know what we hope we will do, but we have no guarantee that's what we will do. Again, look at Peter.

I'm sure he was just as surprised at his behavior as anyone.

"How could I deny Christ?" he no doubt asked himself. "He's my friend. He's my Lord. Yet I denied him again and again and again."

Each of us hopes that we'll make the right decisions, act the right way, do the right thing when faced with temptation, but we can't say for sure what we would do. Those vows that sound so impressive when spoken mean nothing if they can't stand up to the test.

Yet the good news is that Jesus forgave Peter. And when Jesus forgives, he's promised to never remember the transgression. Once we ask forgiveness for our failures, he will never bring them up again. That's one "never" you can count on.

Thoughts to Ponder

Have you ever made a vow, only to later break it?

Why do you think that God would allow our vows to be tested?

Bumper Sticker for the Day
**There are no "Perfect People" lines at the entrance
to heaven.**

Scripture to Stand On

May I never boast except in the cross of our Lord Jesus Christ, through which the world has been crucified to me, and I to the world.

GALATIANS 6:14

Hello Again, Lord ...

Thank you, Lord, for loving imperfect people.

Don't Mention It

I received a Christmas card one year from Paul Brumley, a writer friend of mine. It was a Far Side cartoon that pictured a "fourth" wise man, the one we never hear about because, as the card explained it, "he brought fruitcake to the manger."

I laughed out loud when I read the card. The more I think about it, though, the more I see a parallel to many of us who bring equally unimpressive "gifts" to the Lord. While others are bringing gold, frankincense, and myrrh, we're bringing the fruitcake that's been sitting around our house for years and nobody else wants.

"Church rummage sale? Here, take my shirt. It's OK, really. I want to donate it. I haven't worn it since my dog shredded the sleeves anyway."

"Food drive to feed the hungry? Let's see ... I'm sure there are a couple of cans of garbanzo beans in here somewhere. I hate garbanzo beans!"

"Here comes the offering plate. Now, where'd I put that dollar? It was right here in my wallet with all these twenties, but now I can't find it."

Fruitcake. And the funny thing is, we're proud of our "sacrifices."

"Here you go, Lord," we say, impressed with ourselves. "No need to thank me. It's the least I could do." And we're probably right. It was the least we could do.

Giving, if we're going to do it right, usually involves some degree of sacrifice. It's not what we give that matters, it's what we give in comparison to what we've got. It's what we give in light of how much we could give. Our generosity proves how thankful we are for God's generosity toward us.

If we've been blessed, and most of us have been, maybe we could take another look in our closet to see if we can't find a better shirt to donate. If we've never missed a meal (and dieting doesn't count), maybe there's something other than garbanzo beans that we can give to those who don't know where their next meal is coming from. If we really do hate garbanzo beans, we can certainly give those away, too, but why not add something a bit more substantial to our donation? And when that offering plate comes around, we could probably be a bit more generous there, too. God can certainly use our dollar bills, but if we're giving only the ones and keeping the twenties, fifties, and hundreds for ourselves, then we're not really sacrificing much, are we?

Don't get me wrong. God certainly doesn't resent the fact that we have possessions or that we eat or dress well. The Bible tells us that he's the one who's blessed us with these things anyway. Every good and every perfect gift is from above (James 1:17). He wants us to be blessed. Yet he also wants us to know the blessings that come from giving sacrificially. He wants us to be willing to give him our best. Or to put it another way, he wants more than fruitcake. And if you've ever eaten a fruitcake, especially one of mine, you can't really blame him, can you?

Thoughts to Ponder

Why do you think we tend to bring God our "fruitcake" instead of our best?

Do you think God knows whether our "gifts" have involved any sacrifice on our part?

Bumper Sticker for the Day
God deserves more than our leftovers.

Scripture to Stand On

All they asked was that we should continue to remember the poor, the very thing I was eager to do.

GALATIANS 2:10

Hello Again, Lord ...

Lord, forgive me for the times when I've shown up at your doorstep with fruitcake instead of gold.

Leaving Well
Enough Alone

Have you ever been bitten by a mosquito? Unless you walk around in a mosquito net 24-7, chances are, you have.

Mosquito bites don't hurt all that much at first, but the itching can sure drive you up a wall, can't it? You try everything to stop it—topical antihistamines, oral antihistamines, calomine lotion, and still there's something inside you saying that if you just scratch it a little bit more, it'll feel better.

Yet scratching a mosquito bite will only irritate it. It can even cause the bite to become infected. If you want the bite to heal, the best course of action to take is to medicate the area as best you can, then ignore the bite. In other words, you have to leave well enough alone. If you don't, you'll only make the whole thing worse. One little bite on your wrist can end up making your whole forearm red and swollen.

Some things in our lives need to be left alone so they can heal, too. Hurts, disappointments, bad decisions, poor judgments—they all need healing. Yet if we keep picking at those wounds, if we keep replaying those mistakes until they become irritated, an infection could set in and end up spreading throughout our entire being.

On the other hand, if we receive the right medication (counseling, prayer, etc.) and then leave the wound alone, healing will eventually take place.

Leaving the wound alone, however, doesn't mean that we're in denial that it exists. When a mosquito bites us, we know we've been bitten. The evidence is right there, on our arm or our leg or on the tip of our nose. The deed happened. That mosquito attacked us when we least expected it and it turned us into an all-you-can-eat buffet. It gave little thought to our comfort or well-being. The bites were unprovoked and unwarranted.

Our hurts and disappointments may be unprovoked and unwarranted, too. They may even be unforgivable by the human standard of forgiveness. Maybe we're having a difficult time forgiving ourselves for some mistake we made one, two, even five years ago. Picking at those old "bites" isn't going to help matters, though. It's only going to hurt us and make the situation worse.

So remember—if you don't irritate the hurt, before you know it the hurt won't be irritating you.

Thoughts to Ponder

Do you have a hurt or a past mistake that you keep picking at?

Why do you think it's best to "medicate" that wound with counseling or prayer, then leave well enough alone and allow it to heal?

Bumper Sticker for the Day
Some pains really do go away when you ignore them.

Scripture to Stand On

It is for freedom that Christ has set us free. Stand firm, then, and do not let yourselves be burdened again by a yoke of slavery.

GALATIANS 5:1

Hello Again, Lord ...

Even though it's difficult, help me to leave all those old wounds alone and allow the healing to take place.

Guilty As Charged

Don't want to live under grace? It's your choice. You certainly don't have to. But you should know what that means. It means you're choosing to live under the law. The law? What law?

Read the books of Leviticus and Deuteronomy, just for an example. Now, take out a piece of paper and write down each and every law you see and count up how many times you've broken them in your lifetime. I'd venture to say you'd have quite a long list by the time you were through. We all would.

And that's just the laws from two of the Old Testament books.

Don't want to read all those laws? OK, just take the commandments that God gave to Moses, the ones he etched in stone with his own hand. List them on your paper. There are only ten of them. Now look them over and write down every time you've broken one of these laws. Not just today. Not just yesterday. Review your life from birth to the present, and write down every time you haven't lived up to those ten rules.

Still too much work? All right, just take Jesus' summation of all the commandments, the one where he told us to love God with our whole being and to love our neighbors as ourselves. Make a list of all the times you've broken these two commandments in your lifetime. Even if you only have one entry on your paper (and if you do, you should be applying for sainthood), you have broken the law. The Bible says that if we've broken any of God's laws, we're guilty of all of them.

So you've only told one lie in your lifetime? That's great, but by the law's standards, you're guilty of stealing, too. You've used the Lord's name in vain only once, back in the third grade? That's wonderful, but because you broke one law, you're guilty of idolatry, too. And you're guilty of coveting. And of breaking all the other laws. Break one, guilty of them all. Those aren't my words. They're in the Bible.

Without grace, we're choosing to live under the law and its heavy, heavy hand. Without grace, we're saying we're good enough to line ourselves up with the perfection of Christ. Without grace, we're choosing to stand before God and answer for every single one of our actions, every day of our lives, from birth to death. Without grace, who among us can stand before a holy God?

Don't want to live under grace? Why in the world would any of us want that?

Thoughts to Ponder

Which would you rather do—answer to God for every infraction of his laws or stand before him with a covering of grace?

What does the concept of grace mean to you?

Bumper Sticker for the Day
Grace: Undeserved acquittal. Case dismissed.

Scripture to Stand On

All who rely on observing the law are under a curse, for it is written: "Cursed is everyone who does not continue to do everything written in the Book of the Law."

GALATIANS 3:10

Hello Again, Lord ...

You are a holy and righteous God. Thank you for seeing our many imperfections through eyes of grace.

Heart Problems

Jesus had an issue with people with heart problems. Not the physical kind of heart problems. The spiritual kind. These were people like the Pharisees, who could quote the letter of God's law, but didn't have the compassion of God's heart.

One example of Jesus' encounter with people of this kind is chronicled in Luke 13. It's the account of Jesus healing a woman who had been so sick for eighteen years that she couldn't even stand up straight. The problem, according to the complainers, was that Jesus did it on the Sabbath. Doing any kind of work on the Sabbath was forbidden. Yet, being the kind and compassionate man that Jesus was, and having divine power, he did the good and better thing and healed her.

What did Jesus get for performing this miracle? Did he receive a city council commendation? Did the authorities name a day after him? Was the report of this amazing healing written up in the temple newsletter?

The answer is "none of the above."

The Pharisees and legalistic people of the day saw only the law that was broken. Jesus had "worked" on the Sabbath. They chastised him despite the fact that he had done a good thing and the woman was whole again. They took Jesus to task, citing the law and missing the point.

Jesus knew the law. He hadn't forgotten that "work" was forbidden on the Sabbath. He didn't forget what day it was, either. He knew he was healing the woman on the Sabbath. Yet if anyone knew God's heart, Jesus did. He knew that God would want him to choose compassion over legalism. So he healed the woman and then corrected those who had complained. He called them hypocrites, and then he reminded them that they watered their animals on the Sabbath. Wasn't this woman of as much worth as their animals?

To Jesus, she certainly was.

Thoughts to Ponder

Have you ever been around someone who has cited the "law" in a certain circumstance but missed the point of God's love?

Why do you think Jesus felt he had to confront the legalistic people of his day?

Bumper Sticker for the Day
When love shows up, the prosecution has to rest.

Scripture to Stand On

For in Christ Jesus neither circumcision nor uncircumcision has any value. The only thing that counts is faith expressing itself through love.
GALATIANS 5:6

Hello Again, Lord ...

Heavenly Father, thank you for being a defender of the defenseless.

Wear and Tear

O ne night I was lost, so I pulled into a gas station to ask directions. A lady who was pumping gas and who also happened to be wearing a "What Would Jesus Do?" T-shirt told me how to get to my destination. She was friendly enough, but as it turned out, she gave me the wrong directions.

As I drove around in circles for the next hour, I couldn't help but wonder if that was really what Jesus would have done. Would Jesus have gotten me lost? Would he have told me to turn right when I should have turned left, or to turn left when I should have turned right? His Father created the world. I think he knows his way around it. If I had asked Jesus how to get to where I needed to go, he would have gotten me there. Obviously, the lady didn't intend to give me the wrong directions, but she still got me lost.

I had a good laugh over it, but other encounters with some people sporting witness wear or displaying Christian bumper stickers haven't been so pleasant. We've watched drivers with "Honk if you love Jesus" stickers on their cars cut us off on the freeway. Drivers with "Follow me to church" on their back bumper speed past us going at least twenty miles over the speed limit. How do they expect us to follow them when we can't even catch up? We've seen people with religious jewelry or T-shirts tell off waitresses, store clerks, and anyone else who dared to cross them.

Sporting religious bumper stickers, WWJD bracelets, and

witness T-shirts, or even carrying the Bible, are all good things to do, but we need to think about whom we're representing when we do these things.

Most companies are very careful about the people who represent them. If you're going to be driving around in a company car or wearing a company uniform, the CEO will want you to behave a certain way. If we're going to wear clothing or jewelry or sport bumper stickers on our cars that draw attention to the fact that we're representatives of Jesus, I think it's safe to say he cares about how we represent him, too. He also cares how we act when we're not wearing anything with his name on it.

Thoughts to Ponder

Do you find that you are more conscious of how you act when you're wearing something that indicates you're a person of faith?

Why do you think it's important to always try to be a good representative of Jesus?

Bumper Sticker for the Day
Witness wear needs the witness there.

Scripture to Stand On

Those who want to make a good impression outwardly are trying to compel you to be circumcised. The only reason they do this is to avoid being persecuted for the cross of Christ.

GALATIANS 6:12

Hello Again, Lord ...

Lord, help me to always represent you in the best way I can.

O Patience,
Where Art Thou?

What does it mean to be patient?

It means waiting for your turn at the video arcade while the guy in front of you plays his twenty-seventh consecutive game.

It means not complaining while your little brother tries on his fourteenth pair of shoes at the Vans store.

It means letting Grandpa watch the same episode of *Antique Appraisal* for the seventh time before you ask for the remote control.

It means waiting another twenty minutes for your sister to get off the telephone (and not making monkey sounds on the extension).

It means taking your shower after everyone in the house has used up all the hot water ... and not complaining about the icicles forming on the soap.

It means not honking the car horn when your mom takes forty-five minutes in the grocery store when she said she'd take only ten.

It means waiting to open your locker until after the boy who has the locker below you gets his books, avoiding a confrontation between the edge of the locker and the top of his head.

It means waiting for the "Walk" sign to come on before walking.

It means not taking cuts in the cafeteria lines ... no matter how good the pizza is.

Patience isn't biting your lip or telling someone off under your breath while you wait. It means waiting and not thinking anything at all negative about the situation. You just accept the fact that you need to wait and you do it.

Thoughts to Ponder

In what areas of your life do you find you have the least amount of patience?

Why do you think God made patience a fruit of the Spirit?

Bumper Sticker for the Day
Patience is worth waiting for.

Scripture to Stand On

But the fruit of the Spirit is ... patience.

GALATIANS 5:22

Hello Again, Lord ...

Help me to remember that good things will come to me in time ... if I don't whine.

Go Fish

The other night I walked into my kitchen to get a drink of water, but didn't bother turning on the light. I figured I knew my way around in there, and besides, there was a light shining in from the hallway, so I could see well enough to dodge the kitchen table at least.

After getting the drink and as I turned to leave, I heard a deep, husky voice coming from the dark side of the room.

"What are you lookin' at?" the voice demanded.

All I could do was stand there frozen. Every news alert from the past several weeks ran through my brain.

"Two prison escapees from Texas." No, wait. They already caught those guys. "A serial killer is on the loose ..." No, I think they caught him, too.

The news bulletins went on and on inside my head.

"What are you lookin' at?" the voice in the dark repeated.

I tried to get something to come out of my mouth—a scream, a shout, anything. Yet nothing came. Then, the voice pierced through the darkness again.

"Haven't you ever seen a *talking fish* before?"

A talking fish? No wonder he sounded strangely familiar. It was the fish on a plaque that our son had given his dad for Christmas the year before.

Sometimes we can fear things that have no basis in reality, can't we? In the dark, I was picturing the worst-case scenario. Yet in the light, it was obvious that I had seriously misinterpreted the situation. The truth was that it was nothing more than a rubber fish with a voice box inside it.

When it comes to the gospel, it's important to know what the truth is, too. If someone is trying to make you feel that you're not good enough, that you have to jump through this hoop or that hoop, so to speak, to "earn" God's grace, read and reread the book of Galatians. We can't be good enough to earn it. None of us can. All we have to do is accept it. That's the truth of the situation. Don't stay in the dark about it.

Thoughts to Ponder

Why do you think God wants us to know the truth about his grace?

Has someone ever tried to make you think you had to earn God's grace?

Bumper Sticker for the Day
The best way to preserve truth is without all the additives.

Scripture to Stand On

But even if we or an angel from heaven should preach a gospel other than the one we preached to you, let him be eternally condemned!
GALATIANS 1:8

Hello Again, Lord ...

Thank you, Lord, for the plain truth about your grace.

Playing Dress Up

My brother got married when I was about twelve years old. I hated having to dress up for the wedding. I would have preferred to wear my usual attire—cut-off jeans and a T-shirt.

Yet, like it or not, there I was, all dressed up and more than a little bit wobbly in the new high heels my mom had bought for me. It was the first time I had ever worn high heels, and I hated them, too.

Then, there was the hair. Someone had thought that it would be a good idea to perm my hair that weekend. It was not a good idea. The curl was way too tight, and those two little spit curls on my forehead didn't much help the pillbox hat that I had to wear.

I couldn't believe all that I was having to go through just to look presentable at the wedding. Why couldn't I go the way I usually dressed? Why couldn't I be me?

Evangelist Billy Graham closes his meetings with an old hymn called "Just As I Am." It was written by Charlotte Elliott and William B. Bradbury. Consider some of the words of that song ...

Just as I am, tho' tossed about
With many a conflict, many a doubt,
Fightings and fear within, without,
O Lamb of God, I come. I come.

When we bring our hearts to the Lord, we can come just as we are. We don't have to dress them up. We can come to him with our fears, our doubts, and our conflicts. We get confused sometimes, though, and think that we have to fix everything first.

"Wait until I get my act together, then I'll start serving God."

"God wouldn't want me. Look at everything I've done."

"The church doors would fall over if I ever walked in there."

We put these restrictions on ourselves. They aren't God's restrictions. He just said, "Come." He told us that he's standing at the door and knocking. He said that if anyone hears his voice and opens the door, he will come in. He didn't say, "If anyone hears my voice and is presentable and perfect, then I will come in." He just said that he will come in, mess and all. He knows we can't clean up enough first. There isn't enough soap in the world to clean us up. Or enough fancy clothes. He wants us to come as we are.

Now, if only weddings were the same way.

Thoughts to Ponder

Have you ever felt that you needed to "clean up" first before going to God?

Why do you think God wants us to "come as we are"?

Bumper Sticker for the Day
Soap can't replace grace.

Scripture to Stand On

For all of you who were baptized into Christ have clothed yourselves with Christ.

GALATIANS 3:27

Hello Again, Lord ...

Thank you, Lord, for accepting me.

Free Pass

Does rejecting legalism give us license to do whatever we want contrary to God's Word? Good question. Simple answer—no. Paul clearly explains that our freedom does not mean disorder. In fact, it means just the opposite. The fact that we are free means that we are free to do what's right. We're free to obey God. Instead of obeying him out of fear, though, we obey him out of a sense of gratitude. God tells us in 1 John 5:3a, "This is love for God: to obey his commands."

Don't know what the difference is? Think of it this way—if your parents let you borrow their car for the night (providing you have a license) and they asked you to be home by eleven o'clock, you would probably be home by eleven o'clock. Yet you would also obey some unspoken rules, just out of respect for your parents and their property. You wouldn't purposely drive their car through a car wash with the windows down and the trunk open, right? You wouldn't drive it into your friend's swimming pool, or sell the engine and push the car home. These are things you wouldn't do, not because you're afraid your parents would quit loving you if you did them, but because you love them. You respect them enough to not hurt them unnecessarily. Certainly, you could have an accident, and you would then have to apologize to them for the wrinkled fender, but you wouldn't intentionally go out and have an accident in their car.

That's how we're to be with God, too. We shouldn't want to

intentionally break his laws. We might not think things through and end up making wrong choices and need to ask forgiveness for our behavior, but we shouldn't purposely set out to break God's rules. And even though we don't have to fear losing his love if we fail him, we shouldn't take his love for granted, either. Again, it's a heart issue. That's why Jesus said that the two greatest commandments are that we love God with our whole being and that we love our neighbors as ourselves. If we keep these two commandments faithfully, the others will fall into place.

If we love God, we'll do everything we can to prove it.

Thoughts to Ponder

Do you understand the difference between obeying God out of fear and obeying him out of gratitude for what he has done for you?

Why do you think that God wants your obedience to come from a feeling of gratitude and allegiance rather than from a fear of losing his love?

Bumper Sticker for the Day
Thank God with your life.

Scripture to Stand On

You, my brothers, were called to be free. But do not use your freedom to indulge the sinful nature.

GALATIANS 5:13a

Hello Again, Lord ...

I know I'm not perfect, Lord, but to the best of my ability, may I obey your commandments.

Weapons of Mass Destruction

Ever since the terrorist attack of 9-11, there has been a lot of talk about weapons of mass destruction. We worry about which countries have them, which countries are seeking them, and which countries would use them against us.

As devastating as these nuclear, biological, or chemical weapons are, there's another one that's just as powerful. This weapon isn't mentioned in the news all that often, but it has been a weapon of mass destruction for centuries. It's called discouragement, and it can be pretty destructive. Why?

Discouragement strikes when we least expect it. Ever have a day when everything was going great, then all of a sudden someone came along and said or did something that zapped the joy right out of you? That's called a surprise attack. You don't see it coming and there isn't any time to take cover. That's the way discouragement works. It attacks us when we least expect it and when we're least prepared for it.

When we need encouragement, God doesn't send us discouragement. He doesn't send someone along to say something negative to us, then apologize with "Oops. Maybe I should come back at another time, when you're better equipped to handle this." God knows our hearts. He wants to lift us up, not bring us down. When discouragement strikes, God will often send a counterstrike of encouragement at just the right moment.

No one is immune to the effects of discouragement. Even the people who seem to have everything going for them can get discouraged. Sometimes even more so, because the higher up the ladder you climb, the farther you have to fall. Feelings of self-doubt start kicking in. God wants to promote us, not tear us down. Discouragement isn't his method of operation.

So if you look around and find yourself surrounded by discouragers, don't equate their messages with what God might be wanting to tell you. God will talk to you through his Word. Read it. It's full of encouragement. Enough to last a lifetime.

Thoughts to Ponder

Do you have any discouragers in your life?

What do you think God would want to say to you that's different from the messages of the discouragers?

Bumper Sticker for the Day
God's Word—protective gear against discouragement.

Scripture to Stand On

You were running a good race. Who cut in on you and kept you from obeying the truth?

GALATIANS 5:7

Hello Again, Lord ...

You are my encourager. You lift up my head when I am down. You make me feel better about myself.

Follow the Leader

A fter my niece's high school graduation, the family decided to go out to dinner at a restaurant in the downtown area of Searcy, Arkansas. There were two carloads of us, and I was to follow the lead car. I turned right when they turned right, turned left when they turned left, and went straight when they went straight. I followed every move they made, but became a little concerned when they began driving away from town.

"The restaurant's in town, isn't it?" I asked the others in the car. They all agreed that it was. So why then were we going in the opposite direction?

"They must be taking a shortcut," I said as I continued to follow the red taillights in front of me. One mile, two miles, three miles, I drove, leaving the city and its lights far in the distance behind me. We were now following the lone car in front of us down a very dark road out into the middle of nowhere.

Where in the world were they taking us? If this was any indication of how short their shortcut was, I was going to need more gas.

Yet I drove on, obediently following the other car. Even though I knew, we all knew, that we were going way out of the way, I followed and didn't question. I didn't honk. I didn't flash my lights or wave my hands frantically in an effort to get the other car's attention. I just followed. Blindly. Faithfully.

By now we were miles outside of town. I could no longer see the lights of Searcy in my rearview mirror. I couldn't see any lights at all, no streetlights, no lone farmhouse. Nothing.

I tried speeding up to get closer to the car, but it stayed about ten car lengths ahead of me, and I didn't want to go too fast on that dark, windy, country road.

Finally, another car came around the bend and its headlights clearly outlined the occupants of the car in front of us. Or I should say it outlined the sole person in the car in front of us. Wait a minute ... *one person?* Wasn't there a carload of people in that car? Where'd they all go? How could they have gotten out of the car without our seeing it?

Well, the fact was, they hadn't gotten out of the car. I had somehow lost the car I was supposed to be following and was now following a complete stranger down a dark, lonely road. I had followed that car even though we all knew it was going in the opposite direction of where we should have been going!

We laughed the hardest I think we've ever laughed all the way back to the restaurant.

Have you ever asked yourself who you're following? Did you start out following God, but somewhere along the way you got sidetracked. If you have doubts about the path you're on, you might want to take a closer look at that lead car and make sure the person driving it is the one you should be following.

Thoughts to Ponder

Why do you think it's important to let God have the lead in your life?

Who are you following?

Bumper Sticker for the Day
**If God's in the lead, you won't get a ticket for
following too closely.**

Scripture to Stand On

*This matter arose because some false brothers had infiltrated our ranks
to spy on the freedom we have in Christ Jesus and to make us slaves.*
GALATIANS 2:4

Hello Again, Lord ...

Even when the path gets dark, I won't get lost if I keep my eyes
on you, Lord.

Making the Right Impression

Ernest and Jessie Reeves were an unassuming couple. They were retired farmers who had moved from their Iowa farm to Pharr, Texas, where they lived in a trailer home.

When Mr. and Mrs. Reeves passed away, they left millions to a well-known organization that distributes Bibles around the world. The Reeveses were the largest donors in that organization's history. Friends, neighbors, and fellow church members had no idea that this quiet, humble couple had that kind of net worth. That's because Ernest and Jessie kept their financial affairs, and their overwhelming generosity, quiet.

The Pharisees in the Bible weren't anything like the Reeveses. They wanted everyone around them to know how "spiritual" they were. They said their prayers as loud as they could and bragged about all the things they had done for God. They kept watch as people gave their offerings, and audibly judged those who they felt hadn't given enough. This is the attitude that led them to overlook the widow who had given two mites, not realizing that she had given more than anyone, for she had given all that she had. They did, however, praise those who had given more money, even though their offerings were mere pocket change compared to their great riches.

The Pharisees just didn't get it. They measured their own (and other people's) religion by outward signs. Those who did the things that religious people do, said the things that religious people say, and dressed the way that religious people dress, were the ones who measured up. Anyone else was beneath them.

Yet God looks at the heart. He knows who's real and who's not. He doesn't care about how good a performance we can put on. He cares about the condition of our hearts.

Ernest and Jessie understood this. They knew they didn't have to put on a performance for anyone. Their hearts were right. The only one they needed to impress with their faithfulness was God, so when they gave their gifts to him, they did it quietly and unassumingly.

The Reeveses are both gone now, but the legacy that they've left behind will live on forever. Friends, neighbors, and thousands of people who hear about their story now will know just how generous they were. And something tells me heaven's not keeping that generosity very quiet now, either.

Thoughts to Ponder

Why do you think God wants your religion to be real, instead of an act to impress others?

Why do you think God especially likes the anonymous gifts we give to others?

Bumper Sticker for the Day
When we quit trying to impress others, we'll start impressing God.

Scripture to Stand On

Am I now trying to win the approval of men, or of God? Or am I trying to please men? If I were still trying to please men, I would not be a servant of Christ.

GALATIANS 1:10

Hello Again, Lord ...

God, help me to remember that it doesn't matter who sees my good deeds. You do. And you keep good records.

A Good Harvest

Do you ever feel like it doesn't matter how much good you do, there are some people who will continue to have the attitude, "But what have you done for me today?" Never mind your history of giving and showing kindness to them. That's old news. They want you to do more. And more. And more.

Do you have a job at church that doesn't get a lot of recognition? Do you do it week after week, but hardly ever get a thank you? Do you wonder if anyone even notices or would care if you quit?

Do you help your friends with their homework, and then when you're done, watch them spend all their fun time with someone else?

Do you feel that your good deeds are continually being stepped upon, overlooked, taken advantage of, or discounted altogether?

If you're feeling this way, the Book of Galatians offers encouragement. It tells us that we shouldn't become discouraged when we're doing good deeds for others. Even if they don't see what we're doing, God does. It also says that if we are faithful, the good that we do for others will be returned to us. We'll reap what we've been sowing. If we've sown kindness, we'll reap kindness in return. Maybe not from the same place we've sown it, but from somewhere. If we've sown understanding, we'll reap understanding. Again, it might not come from where we think it ought to come, but it'll come all the same.

So don't get disheartened when the people that you think should be noticing your hard work, your kindness, your love, and your sacrifice, don't. God keeps a good set of books. He knows what you're doing, and he'll make sure that it all is returned to you, in some way, by someone, at just the right time.

Thoughts to Ponder

Is there someone in your life who doesn't show much gratitude for the things you do?

Have you recently had a kindness shown to you by someone from whom you didn't expect it? Do you think you could be reaping one of the seeds of kindness that you've sown?

Bumper Sticker for the Day
Kindness grows where you plant it or where the wind has carried its seeds.

Scripture to Stand On

Let us not become weary in doing good, for at the proper time we will reap a harvest if we do not give up.

GALATIANS 6:9

Hello Again, Lord ...

Sometimes I get tired, Lord, and feel unappreciated. Thank you for your encouragement to keep on doing whatever good I can. I know that you see it all.

Believe It or Not

D o you know someone who is so unsure of his or her own opinion that he or she can't make even the slightest decision?

"Should I buy the red shirt or the blue one? Or how about the green one? Never mind, the yellow one is best, I'm sure of it.... But then again, what do I know? You make the decision for me."

Stand behind someone like this at Baskin Robbins 31 Flavors and you'll never get waited on.

"One scoop of cookie creme and one scoop of strawberry swirl, please.... No, make that one scoop of brownie supreme and one scoop of butter pecan.... OK, I know now. Let's make it two scoops of pistachio cherry and sprinkle some M & M's on top. Wait ... let's go with one scoop of pineapple sherbet and one scoop of French vanilla. Then again ..."

Indecisive people can really get on your nerves, can't they?

Not being able to decide on what flavor of ice cream or which shirt to wear is nothing, though, compared to people who are wishy-washy about what they believe. One day they believe this way, and the next day they believe that way. They carry around the large family Bible until the minute their faith gets challenged, then they run to the other side.

"Bible? What Bible? You must be referring to my history book. They look a lot alike."

They jump from one belief system to the next, and never quite stand for anything.

God wants our faith to be real. Does this mean we can't ask God questions? Does this mean we can't have doubts? Of course not. God can handle our doubts. Could you handle a debate with someone over whether or not you exist? Of course you could. You know you exist, so all the questions in the world aren't going to bother you in the least. Yet when we serve God one day and turn our back on him the next, that's a different issue. That's making a conscious choice to keep him part-time in our lives, and God is a full-time God.

Thoughts to Ponder

Would you say that God is full- or part-time in your life?

Why do you think God doesn't want us to be wishy-washy when it comes to him?

Bumper Sticker for the Day
A double-minded man gets twice the headaches.

Scripture to Stand On

How I wish I could be with you now and change my tone, because I am perplexed about you!

GALATIANS 4:20

Hello Again, Lord ...

Help me, Lord, to have consistent faith.

Taking a Hit

When a soldier falls in battle, his fellow soldiers make every effort to gather him up and get him to safety, realizing his very life might depend on their actions. Sometimes they do so at great personal peril.

When a fellow believer falls, too often we stand by while the enemy continues attacking, or even worse, we join in.

What? We'd never do such a thing!

No? Think about a spiritual leader, gospel singer, or perhaps someone in your own church who has made a mistake in judgment recently. What was the reaction of those around him or her? Did the troops go in and attempt a rescue, no matter what the cost, or did they load their own weapons and start firing rounds of judgment at that person? Or maybe they didn't do anything but turn their backs on the person and leave him or her lying there, wounded and unable to strengthen his or her faith, or fight back.

I have a feeling the reaction to this person's "fall" was mixed. Some probably faithfully stood by him or her, while others began the judgment onslaught, and some just ignored the person and went on about their day.

When fellow believers fall, they need encouragement, not condemnation. They're already condemning themselves. They need to be told of their worth. They're already feeling worthless. They need to be reminded of God's love for them because they probably are asking themselves how he could possibly love them anymore. If we're supposed to be God's army, we should act like true soldiers and rescue our wounded, not shoot them.

One reason we act the way we do could be envy. If we have to hold ourselves to a certain standard, we feel that others should be held to that standard, too. "I can't get away with acting like that. Why should they?" Another reason could be that others' failures remind us of our own vulnerability, and therefore we feel threatened. We're afraid we'll make the same wrong decision someday. Attacking our fallen soldiers can also take the heat off our own failures. We figure if we spend our time pointing out what "they" did, we will never have to face the things that we do that displease God.

God's army cannot fail. Look who we have as our Commander in Chief. There's no way we're going to lose the war. So it's not a matter of weeding out the weakest link so we can win. The Bible tells us that in the end, God will be the victor. Yet wouldn't we look like a better army if we started treating each other, even those who have fallen, like real soldiers, rather than like the enemy?

Thoughts to Ponder

When you hear of fellow "soldiers'" wrong decisions, do you encourage them, reminding them of their worth to both you and God, or do you attack them, either to their faces or behind their backs?

Why do you think God wants us to help our wounded?

Bumper Sticker for the Day
**God doesn't want to court-martial fallen soldiers.
He wants to restore them.**

Scripture to Stand On

Brothers, if someone is caught in a sin, you who are spiritual should restore him gently. But watch yourself, or you also may be tempted.

GALATIANS 6:1

Hello Again, Lord ...

Thank you, Lord, for loving us even after we've taken a hit.

The Gold Circle

Have you ever gotten Gold Circle tickets to a concert? Maybe you had a little extra money to buy them, or you had the right connections. Regardless, it must have felt pretty good to be sitting in that prestigious Gold Circle. Gold Circle seats are the ones closest to the stage; they're premium seats. Some are so close that you can practically reach out and touch the performer. They're the best seats in the house, usually reserved for either the guests of the performer or those of affluence.

Most airlines offer a first-class section for their elite travelers. Again, because of a person's celebrity status, financial standing, or number of frequent flyer miles, he or she can have seats that are separated from the regular passengers. First-class passengers usually get steak for dinner, while the other passengers might be handed a box of crackers, nuts, and an apple. First-class passengers get roomy seats that fully recline, while the other passengers get seats with no legroom and that recline only about an eighth of an inch.

Some hotels offer different classes of service, too. You can either stay in the presidential suite, with a king-sized bed, a kitchen, a grand piano, and a view overlooking the ocean, or stay in a room with a single bed, a radio, and a view overlooking the rubbish container.

Aren't you glad that God doesn't offer his grace on the basis of your notoriety or net worth? There isn't one level for those who earn six figures a year and another level for those who earn six dollars. With God, money, status, and celebrity aren't what separate us into two different lines. It's forgiveness.

There are the forgiven and the unforgiven. There are those who have accepted his free gift of grace, and those who haven't. That's the class separation. Not money. Not fame. Not how good you think you are. Not anything but grace.

Thoughts to Ponder

How does it make you feel to know that God doesn't separate us according to our possessions?

Knowing that God doesn't look at our money, status, or celebrity, how much importance do you think we should be placing on those things?

Bumper Sticker for the Day
When it comes to heaven, it's a matter of who you know.

Scripture to Stand On

As for those who seemed to be important—whatever they were makes no difference to me; God does not judge by external appearance—those men added nothing to my message.

GALATIANS 2:6

Hello Again, Lord ...

Thank you, Lord, for offering a Gold Circle ticket to each one of us.

People Change

"He'll never change."

"There's no hope for her."

"Why waste our time on them?"

"Loser."

Ever feel that way about someone you know? Maybe she's broken eight out of the ten commandments. Maybe this is the fourth time he's tried to change and this is the fourth time he's failed. Why even bother? These kind of people are hopeless, with a capital "H."

Or are they?

Let's look at some of the "hopeless" people who changed after an encounter with the Lord.

First there's the woman at the well. Remember her? She had already been married five times and was currently living with yet another man. That sounds like someone who's made a pretty good mess of her life, wouldn't you say? Yet what did Jesus say to her? Did he dwell on everything she wasn't, or did he dwell on everything that he was? He offered her forgiveness, not more guilt; living water, not condemnation.

What about the woman who was caught in adultery? A crowd had already gathered around her, rocks in hand, ready to stone her to death. I'd say her friends, if she had any, must've thought she looked pretty hopeless. Yet what did Jesus do? Did he walk away and leave her alone?

"I wish I could help, but you've really brought this on yourself, you know."

No. He didn't turn away from her. But wait a minute. She was guilty. The law of that day clearly stated that she was to be stoned.

True. But that was before the God of the hopeless stepped on the scene. Jesus showed the crowd that while she was certainly guilty, they were guilty, too. Maybe not of adultery, but of other things that in God's eyes are just as bad—pride, envy, bearing false witness, gossip, greed. He made the accusers feel their own guilt, then invited any one of them who felt worthy to cast the first stone. No one did, of course, because the only one worthy was Jesus, and he didn't plan to throw any stones.

Hopeless people? They might feel hopeless, and we might see them as hopeless, but they're not hopeless. Not after Jesus steps on the scene.

Thoughts to Ponder

Have you ever thought someone was hopeless?

Do you believe now that God can change that person's heart?

Bumper Sticker for the Day
**Grace covers all sins equally—those of the accused
and those of the accuser.**

Scripture to Stand On

The man who formerly persecuted us is now preaching the faith he once tried to destroy.

GALATIANS 1:23

Hello Again, Lord ...

Thank you, Lord, for being a heart-changer.

Can't We All
Just Get Along?

Do you know that God doesn't approve of discord? Now, just for the record, the word "discord" doesn't refer to the notes that I used to hit during my piano lessons (although some have considered a few of those a sin).

To cause discord means to cause trouble. It's picking up the telephone and telling Friend A something inflammatory about Friend B, then calling Friend C and telling him or her something inflammatory about Friend A, then calling Friend D and ... I could go through the whole alphabet, but you get my drift.

That's causing discord. It's trying to get people to turn against each other. It's being a troublemaker. It's having a mouth that runneth over and not caring who gets drowned in the process.

If you've ever been caught in the middle of a flood like this, you know why God says it's wrong. It can cause a lot of problems for a lot of different people. It can destroy friendships and reputations.

God is a peaceful God. He wants his children to be peaceful, too. He doesn't want us stirring up trouble every chance we get, turning friend against friend, or talking about others behind their backs. He wants us to sow good seeds so that when we reap what we've sown, it'll be something we're proud of.

Thoughts to Ponder

Would you say that you tend to be someone who sows seeds of discord or seeds of harmony?

Since God is listening in on all of your conversations, do you think you're fooling him when you play this game of discord?

Bumper Sticker for the Day
Nothing fragrant can grow from seeds of discord.

Scripture to Stand On

The acts of the sinful nature are obvious ... discord.

GALATIANS 5:19

Hello Again, Lord ...

Thank you for the friends you've added to my life. May I never try to divide them.

Death Row

Have you ever thought, really thought about what Christ did for you?

Imagine yourself serving time on death row. You've been charged, convicted, and sentenced, and now you've run out of appeals. Your death sentence will be carried out. There's not a thing you can do about it. You even petitioned the governor of your state for a stay of execution. He turned you down. It doesn't matter what your crime was, the fact of the matter is that you did it, the court knows you did it, and according to the law, you will be put to death for it.

Now imagine that on the morning of your court-ordered execution, you hear the guards walking down the cement corridor toward your cell. You look through the bars and see a man walking with them. You figure it's some kind of minister or priest coming to give you your last rites.

When they reach your cell, the man prays with you and tells you to be encouraged, and then the guards take him away and tell you that you're free to go.

You stare at the open door in disbelief. You also wonder where the guards are now taking the man. You want to follow, but more than that you want to get as far away from death row as you can before they realize what they've done and change their minds.

As you walk toward the prison gates, past the tower and the armed guards, who have lowered their guns and are waving farewell to you, you notice the prison lights start to flicker. You think it strange because, after all, they've cancelled your execution. Yet you walk on.

Just as you pass through the gate, you see the executioner walk out of the prison and toward the gathered news media. He steps up to the microphone and pronounces that at 10:58 A.M. the capital punishment was rendered. The crowd cheers, then someone notices you standing off to the side. An uproar ensues.

"Wait a minute! There he is!"

"He's breaking out!"

"Stop him!"

The crowd rushes toward you, but the guards hold them back.

"Leave him alone!" they say. "He's a free man."

The warden then steps up to the microphone and raises his hand to quiet the crowd. He explains that in the final hours before the execution, a man had petitioned the court to transfer the crimes to his name and to take your punishment. In a history-making move, the court had granted his wish. At 10:58 A.M. that man was executed in your place.

One by one, the people leave. You overhear their comments:

"Why would anyone die for him?"

"You call this justice?"

"The man must have been insane!"

You wonder the same. Who was that man who had walked down the death row corridor that day? Didn't he know the crimes with which you were charged? Why would he sacrifice himself for someone like you?

The guards close the prison gates, leaving you standing on

the outside, unshackled and free for the first time in eighteen years. Your name has been cleared; your debt to society has been paid. By a stranger. By someone who could have easily joined the crowd, watching you receive the punishment that you deserved. Yet he didn't. Through all your guilt, he saw your worth and he gave you your life back.

Thoughts to Ponder

Knowing what Christ has sacrificed for you, how does it make you feel?

Since he has taken your punishment, in what ways can you show him how much you appreciate what he's done?

Bumper Sticker for the Day
The price of freedom is always great ... to someone.

Scripture to Stand On

Christ redeemed us from the curse of the law by becoming a curse for us, for it is written: "Cursed is everyone who is hung on a tree."
GALATIANS 3:13

Hello Again, Lord ...

Thank you, Lord, for paying the ultimate price for my freedom.

More to the Story

Henry Wadsworth Longfellow once said, "Believe me, every heart has its secret sorrows, which the world knows not; and oftentimes we call a man cold when he is only sad." In other words, that grouch at the gas station may be going through an unwanted divorce; that waitress who was snippy to you over dinner might have a child in the hospital; and that teacher who hasn't smiled all semester could be undergoing cancer treatments. We don't know what challenges people might be facing in their lives. All we see are symptoms. Too often, we jump to judgmental conclusions.

"Geez, what a grouch!"

"What's his problem?!"

"Man, has she got an attitude!"

Waitresses, teachers, store clerks, ushers, that grumpy owner of the video arcade in your town, even your pastor all have personal lives. They're doing their jobs to the best of their abilities, but if they're not as pleasant as you think they should be, try considering the possibility that something else might be going on in their lives.

Not being judgmental means cutting other people some slack. God wants us to be understanding of what others might be facing in their lives. He wants us to try to catch a glimpse of their hearts, the hearts that he sees so clearly.

When Jesus encountered the woman at the well and the woman caught in adultery, he didn't dwell on their string of bad decisions. His heart broke because he saw the sadness in them. He knew there was more to their stories. He knew they needed someone to remind them of their worth, someone to tell them that they were better than what they were settling for. Too often we don't see what God sees in those around us.

We see their rudeness. God sees their emptiness.

We see their anger. God sees their disappointments.

We see their hate. God sees their hurt.

We see their toughness. God sees their fears.

We see their immorality. God sees their lack of self-worth.

We see their demand for attention. God sees their cry for help.

We see their pushiness. God sees their insecurities.

We see their stubbornness. God sees their desperation.

We see their weaknesses. God sees their strengths.

We see their failures. God sees their potential.

We see their past. God sees their future.

Thoughts to Ponder

Think of someone in your life who has been grouchy or mean to you lately. Do you think there could be something else going on in that person's life that might be making him or her act this way?

While personal trials are no excuse to be mean to other people, do you think you could cut this person some slack, realizing that there might be more to the situation than you know?

Bumper Sticker for the Day
A lot of people are screaming for help and not saying a word.

Scripture to Stand On

Carry each other's burdens, and in this way you will fulfill the law of Christ.

GALATIANS 6:2

Hello Again, Lord ...

Help me, Lord, to see others' hurt, not just their hurtful behavior.

Supreme Justice

O nce, while vacationing in Washington, D.C., my family and I visited the United States Supreme Court. It's a beautiful building with steps and massive columns in the front of it. Inside, there are marble floors and pillars, as well as the impressive courtroom where our nine Supreme Court justices sit. If you haven't already had the opportunity to visit this impressive landmark, I hope that you will someday.

The Supreme Court was established to interpret the laws passed by the legislative and executive branches of our government. The nine justices are there to make sure our Constitution is always upheld and that the rights of our citizens are never violated.

From the United States Supreme Court, to the state supreme courts, to the district courts, to the local police precincts, our judges and law enforcement officers are there to make sure that the laws of our nation are followed. Break a law and you could face prosecution and a possible jail sentence. That is, unless the court decides to show mercy. The governor of the state in which the laws were broken also has the option of showing mercy in whichever cases he or she chooses. Even the president can grant a person a presidential pardon. There is no guarantee that you will be afforded such mercy, so I wouldn't recommend breaking the law and testing the system. Still, it is an option that is available to judges, governors, and ultimately, the president.

God, on the other hand, does guarantee us mercy. He promises that once we confess our wrongdoings and ask his forgiveness, he will "remember our sins no more." Even if you're lucky enough to be shown mercy by an earthly court, the record is still there. But with God, the record is put in the heavenly paper shredder, so to speak. It's gone, permanently expunged from your record. That's pretty incredible, isn't it? That's how God's mercy works.

Thoughts to Ponder

Knowing that God puts your past in an eternal paper shredder when you ask for his forgiveness, how does that make you feel?

Does the fact that God is a merciful God make you want to obey his laws or continue to do your own thing regardless of what his love for you has cost him?

Bumper Sticker for the Day
God never forgets, except what he forgives.

Scripture to Stand On

If, while we seek to be justified in Christ, it becomes evident that we ourselves are sinners, does that mean that Christ promotes sin? Absolutely not!

GALATIANS 2:17

Hello Again, Lord ...

Thank you, Lord, for forgiving and forgetting.

No Boundaries

D o you know that God is interested in politics? Not in the
way some of us think he is. He doesn't belong to the
Republican, Democratic, or Green Party, or any other political
party. He may agree with certain aspects of each of them and
disagree with others, but God doesn't completely endorse any
particular political agenda in its entirety. That's because he
has his own agenda.

Even so, God has set up the concept of government so that
we can have orderly societies. Without laws, God knows that
there would be mass confusion. Think about it—what would
it be like to drive with no traffic lights, no stop signs, no speed
limits, no "Do Not Enter" signs, and no "Danger" signs? A lot
of us would end up in head-on collisions, in the ditch, or in
the river, wouldn't we? (Some of us do that even with all the
signs, but at least we've been duly warned.)

What if there weren't any laws, either? You could walk into
your neighbor's house and take anything you wanted, and he
could do the same at your house. And what if murder wasn't
a crime? If someone didn't like the way you happen to part
your hair, they could simply do away with you. I don't know
about you, but I prefer they just recommend a good stylist.

Thank God life isn't like that. We have laws, and we need
them. Laws are necessary because people need boundaries.
Without them, all we would have is chaos.

Now, granted, there are some laws that need to be changed—

old laws that still make it illegal to shoot an elephant in your pajamas, or something equally archaic. Yet in those cases, or in the cases where we strongly disagree with a certain law, there are orderly ways to have that law overturned. Overturning or updating one law, though, doesn't mean we toss them all out.

When the Bible warns us against legalism, it's not saying that we should live in a lawless society. It's simply saying that we need to improve ourselves first before we start trying to improve those around us. We need to see our brother's faults through the filter of our own shortcomings. Why? Because the same measure of mercy that we show to others is the measure of mercy we're going to receive from God for our own failures. So scoop out your mercy with a very big spoon.

Thoughts to Ponder

Why do you think God wants us to be responsible citizens?

Why do you think God wants us to be forgiving citizens, too?

Bumper Sticker for the Day
Laws have a reason. Mercy has a mission.

Scripture to Stand On

Is the law, therefore, opposed to the promises of God? Absolutely not! For if a law had been given that could impart life, then righteousness would certainly have come by the law.

GALATIANS 3:21

Hello Again, Lord ...

Lord, thank you for your laws, but especially for your mercy.

The Whole Truth

Have you ever been placed in the uncomfortable position of having to tell a friend the truth about a certain situation? It's not a fun position to be in, is it?

"You should be careful around Sheila," you warn. "She's not the same friend behind your back that she is to your face."

In your heart you believe you're doing the right thing. You know what you're telling your friend is true. You've heard Sheila say negative things about your friend. You're not repeating gossip. You're simply warning your friend to be careful. You don't want to see her get hurt.

You mean well, but how is your intervention received? Is your friend thankful for the warning, or does the whole thing backfire on you?

Unfortunately, it often backfires.

"I never said anything like that!" Sheila insists.

Now, you know she said those things. She knows she said those things. And God knows she said those things. Yet, somehow, she manages to convince your friend that she didn't. Now, neither one of them will speak to you.

Telling others the truth can be tricky at times, can't it? Sometimes people don't want to hear the truth.

Paul had to face this dilemma, too. He tells us about it here in Galatians. In his letter to the churches of Galatia, he says he's afraid that the same thing will happen to him because he's telling them the truth. He's warning them about people who are trying to get them to turn away from the gospel of grace and to live under a legalistic bondage. He's afraid that they will turn on him for trying to open their eyes.

It's hard to understand why a friend would turn on you just because you told him or her the truth, but it happens. If you've handled it the right way, if you've told your friend directly, without any ulterior motive, then you can feel good in knowing you probably did the right thing. If your friend's safety is in jeopardy, then you absolutely did the right thing.

Yet if your friend turns on you because you've shared a truth with him or her, instead of appreciating what you've done, then just be patient. Sheila, Paul, or whatever name applies in your situation, will eventually be exposed. Your friend will know that he or she chose an imposter friendship over a true one. And when your friend finally does apologize to you, hopefully, you'll be able to show how much of a true friend you really are by forgiving him or her. And even forgiving Sheila.

Thoughts to Ponder

Think of a situation when you felt you had to tell someone a difficult truth. How was it received?

Why do you think some people may not want to hear the truth in certain situations?

Bumper Sticker for the Day
Not wanting to hear the truth doesn't change it.

Scripture to Stand On

Have I now become your enemy by telling you the truth?

GALATIANS 4:16

Hello Again, Lord ...

Lord, help me to know when I need to be honest with someone over a situation, and when that person might need to discover it for him- or herself.

Standard Equipment

Do you know that God enjoys the sound of our laughter? He must. Why else would he have given us the equipment to laugh? God thought the ability to laugh would be so important that he put it in the original design of man. Sort of like the fender on a car. Just as that automobile designer stood back one day and thought, "You know, this is a great creation, but I think it still needs a little something to take some of the shock off a collision." God must have thought the same thing. He must have known that we'd need something to buffer the shock of day-to-day life. So instead of giving us bumpers and shock absorbers, he gave us laughter and joy. It's a good thing, too. A bumper really would have limited the kind of clothes we could wear.

Knowing how important laughter is to life, it's unfortunate that we don't use it more often.

"But life's too serious to laugh about."

That's precisely why we need to laugh ... because life is serious. We all could use a little comic relief.

"Laughter is a waste of time."

Worry is a waste of time. Laughter is almost as important to our well-being as breathing.

"Laughter is disruptive."

Unless your laugh sounds like a moose call, it's not disruptive. What is disruptive, though, is being so immobilized by your fears and problems that you can't accomplish a single thing.

Laughter is healthy. Laughter is powerful. Laughter is healing. And it's a sound that God enjoys.

Thoughts to Ponder

How important do you think laughter is in life?

How many belly laughs would you say you get in any given day?

Bumper Sticker for the Day
Laughter: Music to God's ears.

Scripture to Stand On

But the fruit of the Spirit...is joy.

GALATIANS 5:22

Hello Again, Lord ...

Thank you, Lord, for being a God with whom I can laugh.

Sound Bites

In political arenas, you hear a lot of talk about sound bites. What's a sound bite? Sound bites are those little snippets of a political speech or interview that make good fodder for the evening news and talk shows. They sum up the essence of the speaker's speech or opinion in just a few words.

If the gospel message had to be summed up in sound bites, this is how it might sound:

God created.
Enemy tempted.
Sin entered.
God disappointed.
Judgment rendered.
Man banished.
Mercy needed.
Plan unfolded.
Virgin birth.
World's Savior.
Perfect Son.
Crowd hailed.
Christ betrayed.
Thirty pieces.
Friends hiding.
Nails pounding.
Holy sacrifice.

Guarded tomb.
Risen!
Forgiveness bought.
Grace offered.
Amazing love.

Thoughts to Ponder

What sound bites would you give to the gospel message?

Why do you think it's important to keep the gospel message simple, just as God had intended it?

Bumper Sticker for the Day
The gospel message? God loved.

Scripture to Stand On

We did not give in to them for a moment, so that the truth of the gospel might remain with you.

GALATIANS 2:5

Hello Again, Lord ...

Thank you, Lord, for your simple and incredible message of love.

Too Late

I regret something. It happened about sixteen years ago, but to this day, I still regret it. It was about a week before Christmas. I was standing in line at a local drugstore, awaiting my turn to pay for my purchases. There was only one man in front of me and since he was just buying a few things, I figured it wouldn't take very long.

The clerk rang up the man's total, but apparently, the man didn't have enough cash on him to pay the full bill, so he began looking over his items one by one. Reluctantly, he decided to pass on the greeting card. Handing it back to the clerk, he said, "Here, you can take this off I guess."

The man was clearly disappointed. It was a beautiful card. I couldn't read all of the sentiment written on the card, but it was one of those glittery ones that said something like "To my Wife at Christmas ..."

Feeling sorry for the man, the thought crossed my mind to pay for the card for him, but I was writing a check for my own purchases, so I didn't have the cash on me to just hand him the money. The man would have had to wait until I paid for my own order before he could take his card and leave. Maybe the clerk would just ring it up with my items and let the man go ahead and leave, but there was no guarantee she'd do that. While I stood there going through this scenario and that scenario, debating the pros and cons of each one, the man left.

The clerk placed the card back on the counter and proceeded

to ring up my order. I thought about going ahead and buying the card just in case the man was still in the parking lot when I walked out there, but decided not to. Surely, the man would be long gone by the time my order was completed.

Now, buying a Christmas card for that man's wife was certainly his own responsibility. He could have easily put one of his other items back and bought the card himself. For whatever reason he chose not to. Yet I still felt bad for him, and have never forgotten that incident, no matter what other good deeds I've tried to do over the years. Why? Because God had placed in my path that particular person, who no doubt needed an unexpected blessing that Christmas. Yet while I was trying to figure out the best way to deliver my good deed, the opportunity passed.

Thoughts to Ponder

Have you ever missed an opportunity to do something nice for someone?

Why do you think it's important to be aware of the opportunities to do good that God sends your way each and every day?

Bumper Sticker for the Day
Opportunity knocks, but it won't knock the door down.

Scripture to Stand On

Therefore, as we have opportunity, let us do good to all people, espe-cially to those who belong to the family of believers.

GALATIANS 6:10

Hello Again, Lord ...

Lord, thank you for the opportunities you give us every day to help me make someone else's day a little nicer.

Fan Clubs

Are you a sports fan? Do you have a favorite basketball, baseball, or football team? My youngest son, Tony, loves football and is an avid Kansas City Chiefs fan. He tries his best to watch every single game they play during football season. He cheers when they win and groans when they lose. He's got Kansas City Chiefs clothing, bumper stickers, and even a Kansas City Chiefs mouse pad. Our good friends, Sam and Darlene Mehaffie, once invited him to fly out to Kansas City and go to a Chiefs game with them. Tony loved it, of course. Yet even though there was the added excitement of being at a live game, Tony wasn't any more dedicated to the Chiefs there in Kansas City than he had been all along. He's a die-hard Chiefs fan, whether he's at home or standing in the stands at the Chiefs' home stadium.

The apostle Paul is telling the churches of Galatia that their enthusiasm is good, as long as it's for the right purposes, but that they shouldn't be zealous only when he is with them.

Have you ever been that way with your youth pastor?

"Is there anything I can do to help?"

"Why don't I set up the sound equipment tonight? It'll give you a break."

"Do you need anyone to make phone calls for you? I'm free tomorrow afternoon."

That sounds great on the surface, but then as soon as his back is turned,

"Why doesn't anybody else help out?"

"Why do I always get stuck with the grunge labor?"

"I'm always doing everything. Why doesn't anyone else ever volunteer?"

Paul didn't want to be surrounded by fellow believers who were zealous for God's work one minute and complaining about it the next. He needed believers who were consistent. Believers who didn't need to have someone always looking over their shoulder to make sure they were doing what they needed to be doing. And although it's certainly easy to see why the church would be more excited when Paul was in their midst (he'd be the ultimate guest speaker), Paul wanted to make sure that the people were committed to carrying on their mission whether he was with them or not. He wanted them to be true fans of the gospel.

Thoughts to Ponder

Does your commitment to God's work change depending on whom you're talking with?

Would you say God's team deserves your total commitment, wherever and with whomever you happen to be?

___

Bumper Sticker for the Day
When it comes to your commitments, don't be a quick change artist.

___

Scripture to Stand On

It is fine to be zealous, provided the purpose is good, and to be so always and not just when I am with you.

GALATIANS 4:18

Hello Again, Lord ...

Lord, help me to be a good person, not just a good actor.

On Top

Ambition is a good thing. It's what gets you out of bed in the morning after your alarm clock rings. It's what makes you study for your finals. It's what drives you to practice and practice and practice so you'll make the basketball team. It's what makes you put in the necessary time learning to play the guitar, the piano, or the tuba. It's what drives you to succeed. Ambition is a positive force in life.

Selfish ambition isn't positive, however. Selfish ambition is what drives you to step all over your competition in order to achieve. It's what makes you set your brother's alarm clock back an hour so he'll miss the football tryouts and you won't. It's what makes you ask a teacher's aide for the answers to a test. It's what helps you get what you want, but not in a way that would make most people proud.

Selfish ambition is wrong. Paul is telling us here that we're not to climb to the top of the ladder while stepping on the fingers of others. He's telling us not to trip the runner next to us and then smile innocently as we receive our prize. He's telling us to run the race, but to play fair.

God wants us to achieve great things in our lives. Most of us don't have any concept of all that God has in store for us. He had great plans for Moses. He had great plans for David. And he has great plans for you and me. Don't ever think that God meant for us to be humble losers. Far from it! He wants us to be humble winners! Think about it—God is a God of great achievement. Look what he did with the world. He made something pretty incredible out of nothing. So, he obviously endorses achievement. He just wants us to recognize where all of our achievement comes from, and he wants to be proud of the way we accomplish whatever we accomplish in life.

Thoughts to Ponder

Why do you think it's important to God how you handle your achievements?

Do you think it feels just as good to win something by selfish ambition as it does to win something by true ambition?

Bumper Sticker for the Day
He who steps on other people will have a bumpy path.

Scripture to Stand On

The acts of the sinful nature are obvious ... selfish ambition.
                                          GALATIANS 5:19-20

Hello Again, Lord ...

Help me to fulfill the plans you have for my life, Lord, and to do it the right way.

Wah!

Have you ever seen a two-year-old throw a temper tantrum? A real big one. One of those where the kid falls on the floor in the middle of the store, kicks his feet, and screams at the top of his lungs until not only everyone in the store can hear him but everyone in the county! And what's it usually over? It's not over the state of the world today. It's not over the economy. More often than not, it's because something didn't go that child's way. She wanted to walk, but her parents wanted her to ride in the cart. He wanted a toy, but his parents said no. She wanted a certain kind of cereal, but her parents wanted to buy oatmeal instead. (OK, maybe that justifies a little protest, but nothing like what I have just described.)

Temper tantrums are pretty self-focused, aren't they? The one throwing the tantrum doesn't really care who's looking at him, who's hearing him, or who's having to put up with his behavior.

And when the child's mother or father tries to pick him up and carry him out of the store, often the kid starts kicking and flailing, not really caring whom he hurts, either.

That's two-year-old behavior. It's not good two-year-old behavior, but it's certainly childish behavior.

As children grow into adolescents and adults, however, those kind of temper tantrums are supposed to go away. Somewhere along the line, we should learn that tantrums don't really get us anywhere. Nobody else should have to listen to us wail because we didn't get our way.

"But I wanted those new jeans! WAH!"

"I have to go to that party! WAH!"

"I don't wanna clean my room! WAH!"

Now, granted, maybe we really did want those new jeans. Maybe we wanted to go to the party. Maybe our room was a terrible mess and we feared for our safety if we had to go in there and clean it. Our feelings aren't the problem. They're natural. The problem comes when we throw the tantrum.

Paul is telling us here that fits of rage are wrong. They're a sign of a lack of control. They're a sign of selfishness. And in adulthood, fits of rage can often be a sign that something else is going on inside the individual that has little to do with the new jeans, the party, or the messy room. Yet if we ask God to heal the broken part of us, our rage can be replaced with God's peace, and our disorder will become order. The bedroom, though, might take a little longer.

Thoughts to Ponder

Are you, or is someone you know, prone to fits of rage?

What do you think is the true reason behind these temper tantrums?

Bumper Sticker for the Day
People who easily boil over usually make a mess of things.

151

Scripture to Stand On

The acts of the sinful nature are obvious ... fits of rage.
GALATIANS 5:19-20

Hello Again, Lord ...

Lord, heal those places in my life where I'm harboring hurt.

For a Change

D o you know that people are watching your life? I'm not talking about the FBI, private investigators, prowlers, or anything like that. I'm talking about those around you—your friends, your neighbors, and your family. People are watching to see how you'll react in certain situations. They're watching to see if you'll stay faithful to the God you say you love. They're watching to see if you truly trust the God you say you trust. They're watching to see if you take your commitment to your faith seriously.

It's easy for us to get self-focused and to think that whatever happens in our lives is affecting only us. We can tell ourselves that it's our business and that we can react however we want to react. Yet if we want those around us to take our faith seriously, then what we're saying has to match up with what we're living.

Paul's life matched up with his talk. When he went from being a persecutor of the church to being a believer, he knew he was sure to have his share of skeptics. It wasn't going to be easy for people to accept that Saul was now a completely new person. Saul had quite a reputation to overcome, and even though he'd had a life-changing experience on the road to Damascus, and even changed his name, he knew there were plenty of people who were wagering on whether his conversion was true.

Yet it was true, and Paul's life backed it up. His life proved he was a believer in Christ. It proved that he was a champion of grace. It proved that the change was real.

Those who watched this transformation were encouraged in their own struggles, just as those who watch your life are encouraged when your walk matches your talk.

Thoughts to Ponder

Would you say that more often than not your life is an encouragement to those who are watching you?

If you knew Paul when he was Saul, would you have been skeptical of his conversion, or would you have accepted his word that he had changed?

Bumper Sticker for the Day
If your life were a reality show, what would people learn from it?

Scripture to Stand On

And they praised God because of me.

GALATIANS 1:24

Hello Again, Lord ...

Lord, help me to live my life so others will be encouraged because of it.

Challenges

One thing that most handicapped people will tell you is that they want to be treated like everyone else. They don't want to be shunned, or stared at, or made to feel less than any other human being. They're regular people just like you and me. We all have challenges.

Whether our challenges are physical, economical, emotional, or social, we all want to be treated with respect, understanding, and equality. We don't want to be avoided. We don't want to be made to feel helpless. We don't want to be made to feel different. We want to be treated like the complete and unique human beings that we are.

Paul appreciated this kind of treatment, too. Here in Galatians, he thanks the people for welcoming him into their hearts in spite of his illness. It doesn't really matter what kind of an "illness" Paul suffered from. We know that he had some sort of physical challenge, but the people of the churches of Galatia didn't let that challenge affect how they treated Paul. They didn't shun him or make him feel inferior because of it. Paul appreciated this and thanked them for it.

We never know who God is going to put in our path. The Bible says in Hebrews 13:2 that we shouldn't neglect to be hospitable to strangers because by doing so, "some have entertained angels unaware." Paul wasn't an angel, but he was a messenger of God, and thankfully, the churches of Galatia did not let Paul's "illness," keep them from hearing his message.

Thoughts to Ponder

Are there some challenges that you have to face in life?

How does it make you feel when someone sees your value, instead of your challenge?

Bumper Sticker for the Day
Life's tough, but God's enough.

Scripture to Stand On

Even though my illness was a trial to you, you did not treat me with contempt or scorn. Instead, you welcomed me as if I were an angel of God, as if I were Christ Jesus himself.

GALATIANS 4:14

Hello Again, Lord ...

Thank you, Lord, for the challenges that are in my life. They have helped make me the person I am.

Do I Have To?

Why do I have to go mow the lawn? I always have to do it. Make someone else do it this time."

"Get you a glass of water? Can't you get it yourself? It's right over there."

"Go to the store for some bread? My show's on. Tell someone else to do it."

Ever feel like this when someone asks you to do something?

Sometimes others' requests can seem unfair, can't they? Maybe you do always have to mow the lawn. Maybe the water is "right over there" and they could easily get up and get it themselves. Maybe you've been waiting all week to watch your show, did your homework early just so you would be able to sit down and enjoy it, and now someone's asking you to go to the store to get some bread. It's aggravating, isn't it?

Paul wants us not just to "serve one another," but to do it in love. This means that if you're going to go out and mow the lawn, you won't stomp your feet and grumble under your breath all the way out the door. If you're going to get up and get your brother or sister a glass of water, you won't bark at him or her as you do it. If you're going to miss your television show and go to the store to get that bread, you won't make everyone pay for your sacrifice by having to listen to your complaining. Do the good deed, but do it with a loving attitude.

In most instances in life, there is room for compromise. If

you don't complain, maybe your mom will let you go to the store after your show. If not, maybe you can videotape your show and watch it later. If you really do have to mow the lawn more often than your siblings do, maybe you can point that out to your parents and work out a compromise. If you get your brother or sister a glass of water, maybe he or she will get you one the next time you don't want to get up and get it yourself.

Most resentment stems from a feeling of not being heard. If you learn to speak up, at the right time and in the right way, compromises are often made and unfair situations improve.

Serving one another is something that God wants us to do. Yet he wants us to do it cheerfully and in love. Not grumbling and in aggravation.

Thoughts to Ponder

Is there a situation in your life that you feel is unfair and that you might need to talk with someone about?

If you never let your feelings be known (in the right way and at the right time), is it fair to assume that others know your view on the matter?

Bumper Sticker for the Day
God wants us to be full-service, not self-serve.

Scripture to Stand On

... rather, serve one another in love.

GALATIANS 5:13b

Hello Again, Lord ...

Give me the power to always go the extra mile, even when I'm almost out of fuel.

Limit Lines

Have you ever been three days into a diet only to have a Ben and Jerry's commercial come on the television screen, tempting you to try a helping of their delicious ice cream? It takes a lot of self-control not to get up and go to the freezer and scoop out a casserole dish full of Chunky Monkey, doesn't it?

Have you ever been in the position of having a perfect view of your classmate's test paper, the one who usually gets straight A's on tests? It takes a lot of self-control not to take advantage of the opportunity, doesn't it?

Have you ever been alone with your boyfriend or girlfriend and been tempted to get a little closer than you know you should? It takes a lot of self-control to put on the brakes and decide to go somewhere else, where other people will be around, thereby removing the temptation.

It takes self-control to resist these and other kinds of temptations, doesn't it? So where does self-control come from? Paul tells us here that self-control is one of the fruits of the Spirit. It's something that God gives us to help us in life. With self-control we'll have more power to say no to that scoop of ice cream when we know we're full and don't really need the extra calories. With self-control we'll have a pressure valve that will keep us calm and counting to ten, instead of losing our temper. Self-control will also help us set limit lines when it comes to our boyfriends or girlfriends. And self-control will keep our eyes on our own papers during tests.

It's been said that character is who you are when no one is looking. That's when the real you comes out. Self-control helps you make that real you the best you possible.

Thoughts to Ponder

Do you feel you have enough self-control?

Why do you think self-control is important to your physical, emotional, and spiritual maturity?

Bumper Sticker for the Day
True character is found when no one's around.

Scripture to Stand On

But the fruit of the Spirit is ... self-control.

GALATIANS 5:22-23

Hello Again, Lord ...

Thank you, Lord, for helping me to stay within your limit lines.

Return to Sender

Have you ever heard the saying "What goes around, comes around"? That doesn't refer to a hula-hoop contest or a merry-go-round at some amusement park. It's talking about the things that we say or do and how they'll come back to us someday. In other words, if we show someone a kindness, that kindness will eventually be returned to us. It might not be returned by the same person (and often it isn't), but somehow, in some way, through somebody, it will come back to us.

By the same token, if we are unkind to people, that unkindness has a tendency to show up on our doorstep, too.

Remember the story of the unmerciful servant in the Bible? He was forgiven a great debt, but instead of passing along that kindness and keeping the flow of good things happening in his life, he passed along selfishness and a complete lack of mercy. He refused to forgive someone else who owed him a much smaller debt. And what happened? The unmerciful servant's debt was reinstated and he was thrown into jail.

What goes around, comes around.

We can influence how much good comes our way in life by freely offering kindness, love, friendship, understanding, mercy, acceptance, and forgiveness to others. We can also influence how much unkindness, hate, judgmentalism, unforgiveness, and exclusion comes our way by giving these attitudes to others.

In other words, if we want to have more kindness shown to us, we need to show more kindness to others. If we'd like more generosity shown to us, we need to show more generosity to others. If we want to receive more love, we need to give more love to others. And so on. And so on. Again, it might not be from the same person, but somehow, in some way, through somebody, what we give out will come back to us.

Thoughts to Ponder

Would you say you spend more time sowing seeds of kindness and mercy, or sowing seeds of judgmentalism and exclusion?

Can you think of a time when the kindness that you showed someone was returned to you through someone else?

Bumper Sticker for the Day
What goes around, comes around. So rejoice or get ready to duck.

Scripture to Stand On

The one who sows to please his sinful nature, from that nature will reap destruction; the one who sows to please the Spirit, from the Spirit will reap eternal life.

GALATIANS 6:8

Hello Again, Lord ...

Lord, help me to sow the kinds of seeds that I want to harvest

Hate Ain't So Great

Have you ever hated someone? Really hated someone? Maybe that person hurt you. Maybe he or she hurt your family. Maybe he or she was as mean as mean could be and you didn't deserve any of it. Maybe you feel totally justified in your hatred. Maybe you feel hating this person is the only thing you can do under the circumstances.

But then along comes Jesus ...

Jesus has a different take on hatred. He tells us that when someone hurts us, we need to pray for that person. Not hate. Not get even. Pray. That's pretty revolutionary, isn't it? Praying for our enemies. Imagine that!

Yet that's asking the impossible, isn't it? How can he possibly expect us to pray for that person who was so mean to us? How can he ask us to pray for someone we simply cannot stand? How can we pray for someone who doesn't deserve our prayers?

Well, Jesus didn't say it would be easy. He just told us to do it. It's important to note, though, that Jesus didn't tell us to pretend what happened didn't happen. We know it happened. The other person knows it happened. And God knows it happened. Burying our heads in the sand about the incident isn't healthy. Recognizing the hurt and giving it over to God is.

God knows and cares about every one of our hurts. We can't hide them from him. Yet he wants us to talk to him about the situation. He wants us to know that he understands exactly what we're going through. Don't forget, people were mean to him, too. He's felt many of the same feelings we might be feeling, and he wants to encourage us in whatever we're going through. But he can't do that unless we talk to him about it.

Pray for our enemies? If we'd only start doing that, not only would the hate go away, but so would the hurt.

Thoughts to Ponder

Do you have feelings of hatred toward someone in your life?

Even if you feel fully justified in your hatred, do you think that Jesus might be wanting you to talk to him about it so that the healing may begin?

Bumper Sticker for the Day
Harboring hatred will always sink your ship.

Scripture to Stand On

The acts of the sinful nature are obvious...hatred.

GALATIANS 5:19-20

Hello Again, Lord ...

I know that you're not asking me to be a doormat for my enemies, Lord. Just a friend.

Overwhelmed

T hroughout my life I've been blessed to have some incredible kindnesses shown to me and my family. Too many to ever list here. Far more than those instances when people have been less than kind.

It would take more than a book to thank all the people that I need to thank. Once when we were living through some lean years, our pastor came over and gave us fifty dollars. Not out of a love offering taken from the congregation, or out of some special fund set up by the church board, but out of his own pocket. We know it was a gift direct from God's heart because this pastor had no way of knowing the situation we were in or that we truly didn't know where our next meal was coming from.

I once had a lady come up to me in the middle of a difficult situation that I was going through and say that God had told her to remind me that he loved me. She'll never know just how much her encouragement meant to me that day.

I've received countless letters from readers who have written just to encourage me, to tell me how much they've enjoyed my work, and to say they're praying for me. Often those letters come at the precise moment I need them. (As most encouragement does.)

All of these kindnesses—kindnesses that were shown to my husband and I, kindnesses that were shown to our sons at times in their lives when they needed encouragement—are locked away in my memory.

It takes time to write a letter and encourage someone.

It takes an effort to get up out of your seat, walk over to

someone, and say something uplifting. It takes sacrifice to give to someone in his or her hour of need. Yet God sees each and every act of kindness that we do. And believe me, the people on the receiving end never forget it.

Thoughts to Ponder

Think about an act of kindness that someone has shown you. Do you think that person has any idea what that act of kindness truly meant to you? If not, why not write or call that person today to tell him or her?

Is there someone in your life who could use an act of kindness this week?

Bumper Sticker for the Day
Kindness always has perfect timing.

Scripture to Stand On

But the fruit of the Spirit is ... kindness.

GALATIANS 5:22

Hello Again, Lord ...

I am so thankful for the kindnesses that have been shown to me and to my family. Help me to always be willing to pass those kindnesses on to others.

Inheritance

Do you know that as a child of your parents, you have certain rights? Unless you ride your skateboard over the sprinkler and bust the pipe that floods the yard that loosens the foundation that shifts your house and gets it condemned and your parents end up writing you out of their will, you have the right to inherit your parents' estate simply by being their child. (So maybe you better be a little more careful about where you ride your skateboard!)

When God sent Jesus to the earth, his sacrifice on the cross bought our redemption and gave us full rights as sons of God. God is our Father. Think about that. Our "Dad" created the world. Our "Dad" owns every river, every ocean, every mountain we've ever seen. Our "Dad" can take on anyone who might mess with us. Our "Dad" will never walk out on us. Our "Dad" won't miss a birthday, a graduation, or a soccer game. He will be there for us whenever we need him. Our "Dad" is pretty awesome!

Being a child of God is better than being the child of a millionaire, a movie star, or even the president. Inheriting eternal life is better than inheriting a ten-thousand-acre farm, a million dollars in stock, or the biggest mansion on earth. Being a child of God is better than being the child of the toughest fighter in the boxing ring. It's better than being born at Buckingham Palace. As one of his heirs, you're guaranteed a life beyond anything you could ever imagine. Will it be painless?

Not always. Will it bring fame? Not necessarily. Will you have connections? You can't get more connected. Will there be perks? Too many to count. How about wealth? In inner peace and joy, absolutely!

God is your Father. Think about that. And never forget it.

Thoughts to Ponder

How does it make you feel to know the kind of Father you have?

In what ways do you think that you could be a better son or daughter to him?

Bumper Sticker for the Day
Don't write yourself out of God's will.

Scripture to Stand On

You are all sons of God through faith in Christ Jesus.

GALATIANS 3:26

Hello Again, Lord ...

Thank you, Father, for the inheritance you have given to all your children.

Previous Lives

Do you know that when you become a believer, everything changes? It's like God takes all those broken parts of your heart and life and puts them back together again. He takes all the wrongs you wish you could make go away, and he deletes them. They're gone. History. He doesn't remember them even if you keep bringing them up.

Look at what Paul's life was like when he first came to Jesus. He himself confesses that he used to be a persecutor of the church. Think about that for a minute. If Saul (that was his name before God changed his heart) were alive today, he'd be making the rounds on all the news talk shows, making fun of Christians. He'd be standing outside our church services, challenging everyone's faith in Jesus. He'd be ridiculing us, he'd be persecuting us, he'd be someone we would not like very much, right?

But then God changed Saul's heart, and he became Paul. He no longer persecuted the church, and in fact he became passionate for it. He no longer made fun of believers, but instead became one of their leaders. His whole attitude about Jesus changed. Miraculously. And completely.

It doesn't matter what you've done in your past, God can change your heart, too. He won't remember the things you've said against him, or the things you've done that have hurt him; he'll just give you a brand-new start. He doesn't hold grudges. He doesn't keep your old records on file, just in case he needs

170

to "bring them up again." He destroys them. You can't retrieve them. They're gone. They're history. They're forgiven.

Thoughts to Ponder

How does it make you feel to know that when God forgives your past, he forgets it?

If your life were suddenly a clean slate from this day forward, what would be the first thing you would want to write on it?

Bumper Sticker for the Day
When God "deletes," it's complete.

Scripture to Stand On

Before this faith came, we were held prisoners, by the Law, locked up until faith should be revealed.

GALATIANS 3:23

Hello Again, Lord ...

Thank you, Lord, for your forgiveness ... and your "delete" key.

That's My Dad

There's something about a good father.

He loves his children even when they're acting unlovable.

He's proud of them even when they're falling short of their potential.

He hopes they'll make the best decisions for their lives, but gives them the freedom to make them, right or wrong. He knows that's the way they'll mature.

He's always gentle in handling their feelings.

He never withholds his love.

He'll come to their rescue when they need him.

He'll defend them when they're accused.

He'll encourage them.

He's never too tired or too busy or too important to spend time with them.

He can always be counted on.

He never misses a chance to cheer them on.

He loves them enough to die for them.

He thinks about them day and night.

They mean everything to him.

It's like the little girl who walks to school every day and thinks that the sun is her own personal spotlight. And in a way, it's true. It is her own personal spotlight, and it's yours and mine, too. The sun shines on each one of us individually, and on the world as a whole, reminding us how much we mean to

God. We have his undivided attention. We have his admiration and love.

So the next time you feel the sun shining on you, think of it as God's spotlight. Then say to yourself, "That's my Dad. He's just reminding me how much he loves me."

Thoughts to Ponder

How does it make you feel when you think about how much you mean to God?

What can you do today to show God how much you appreciate him?

Bumper Sticker for the Day
Good fathers never give up on their children.

Scripture to Stand On

Because you are sons, God sent the Spirit of his Son into our hearts, the Spirit who calls out, "Abba, Father."

GALATIANS 4:6

Hello Again, Lord ...

Thank you, Father, for not giving up on me.

No Limitations

U pon being honored at an awards ceremony, legendary comedian Jack Benny once said, "I don't deserve an award, but I have arthritis and I don't deserve that either."

It's a funny line, but when we get sick or have a physical limitation of some kind, we really don't deserve it, do we? No one does. No one deserves to have physical, social, or intellectual limitations imposed upon him or her. We'd much rather have the full use of our bodies. We'd much rather have plenty of money. We'd much rather have an IQ of 140 or above.

Not all of us do. So what can we do about it? We can make the best of what we have.

There are people with high IQs doing absolutely nothing worthwhile with all that knowledge. There are people with perfectly healthy bodies putting the poison of illegal drugs into them every day. There are people with as much money as they could possibly want doing nothing that has any eternal value with their money.

It's not what you have. It's what you do with it.

It was Paul's illness that enabled him to bring the gospel to the Galatians. That's what he tells us here. It wasn't his intellect. It wasn't his money. It was his illness. That's what opened the door for him to minister to them.

That very thing that you think would hold you back could be the very thing that God wants to use to move you ahead.

Thoughts to Ponder

Do you have a limitation that you wish you didn't have?

Do you think God might have a plan to use that very limitation for his purpose someday?

Bumper Sticker for the Day
We've put the limit in limitation. God hasn't.

Scripture to Stand On

As you know, it was because of an illness that I first preached the gospel to you.

GALATIANS 4:13

Hello Again, Lord ...

Lord, thank you for using me just as I am.

Gentle on My Mind

There was a lady in the church I used to attend who made an unforgettable impression on me. Was it her clothes? Her singing? The way she could play the piano?

No. None of the above.

It was her gentleness.

This lady wasn't in charge of any program, she didn't teach a Sunday school class or do anything that was very high profile. She just faithfully attended each and every service, sitting quietly in the middle of the left-hand section of the church. If you didn't know her, you probably would walk right past her. Yet faithfully she sat there week after week, quietly praying for others, gently encouraging everyone to whom she spoke, and being more of a blessing than she'll ever know.

We don't hear a lot about gentleness these days. When we need a speaker, we ask the one with the best stage presence and most powerful message. If we need a soloist, we ask that choir member with the unbelievable voice. If we need someone to help with the youth on Friday nights, we ask someone with a lot of energy and a big car.

Gentleness? We don't seek out that quality in others very often do we?

"She's not bold enough."

"He's too quiet."

"She's too much of a pushover."

"He's way too easy."

However, a gentle spirit isn't a weakness. It's a fruit of the Spirit. It's a quality that Christ had. And we should have it, too.

The gentle lady I'm talking about has since moved away. So have I. I no longer see her every Sunday, but I'll forever remember her kindness to my family and me. I'll remember her prayers. And I'll remember her gentle spirit.

Thoughts to Ponder

Do you think that gentleness is a positive or a negative attribute?

Why do you think God listed gentleness as a fruit of the Spirit?

Bumper Sticker for the Day
An ounce of gentleness does more good than a ton of condemnation.

Scripture to Stand On

But the fruit of the Spirit is ... gentleness.

GALATIANS 5:22-23

Hello Again, Lord ...

Thank you for the gentle people who have crossed my path.

Pray Before You Speak

Have you ever had to confront someone over something that he or she was doing? How did it make you feel? Were you excited about finally having the chance to "straighten that person out"? Did you call up your friends afterward and tell them every juicy detail of the encounter? Did you feel happy that at long last this person was put in his or her place?

Or did the whole idea of confronting this person send you to your knees, begging God to assign the task to someone else, or to hurry up and change the other person's heart so a confrontation wouldn't be necessary?

Confronting people isn't an easy thing to do. It's not supposed to be. If it comes easily to you, you might want to take another look at your motives and your heart.

If you're looking forward to confronting someone, to putting that person in his or her place, chances are your mission isn't coming from God. Look at how the prophets in the Bible reacted when they had to confront those who were acting contrary to how they should have been acting. The prophets agonized over the confrontations. They prayed, they fasted, and they would rather have done anything else than to be the one to undertake the confrontation.

Certainly there are times when we have to confront people. When a situation is adversely affecting our spiritual, mental, or physical well-being, or the spiritual, mental, or physical well-being of others, those responsible need to be confronted.

When we do, however, we need to pray first. We need to speak what God wants us to say, not what we want to say. We need to speak to those being confronted privately and respectfully. And we need to have the sincere hope of improving the situation, not just of getting in our two cents' worth.

Thoughts to Ponder

Have you ever had to confront someone over a certain situation?

What was your attitude before, during, and after the confrontation? Do you feel it was a godly one?

Bumper Sticker for the Day
Being right doesn't give us permission to act wrong.

Scripture to Stand On

I went in response to a revelation and set before them the gospel that I preach among the Gentiles. But I did this privately to those who seemed to be leaders, for fear that I was running or had run my race in vain.
GALATIANS 2:2

Hello Again, Lord ...

Lord, when I need to confront someone, help my heart and my motives to be aligned with your way.

Promises, Promises, Promises

D o you know that God by his very nature can't break his promises?

Maybe your dad promised to show up at your basketball game but went golfing instead.

Maybe your little brother promised to do your chores if you helped him clean his room. But you did and he didn't.

Maybe your mom promised to buy you that new CD you've been wanting, but then she said she didn't have the money, as she rushed to make her nail appointment.

It hurts to have promises made to us broken, doesn't it? When people promise us something, we eagerly anticipate that they're going to keep their word. When they go back on it, it's disappointing.

Yet by his very nature, God can't break his promises. When he makes a covenant with us, he simply can't go back on his Word. Whatever he's promised in his Word is ours. We can take it to the bank, so to speak.

So let's look at some of the promises that God has given to us.

For God so loved the world that he gave his one and only son that whoever believes in him shall not perish but have eternal life.

JOHN 3:16

If you remain in me and my words remain in you, ask whatever you wish, and it will be given you.

JOHN 15:7

I am with you always, to the very end of the age.

MATTHEW 28:20

When God makes a promise, he sticks to it. When God makes a promise, you can count on it. When God makes a promise, he won't let you down.

Thoughts to Ponder

How does it make you feel when someone breaks a promise?

How does it make you feel to know that God can't break his promises?

Bumper Sticker for the Day
When you want someone who won't let you down, look up.

Scripture to Stand On

Brothers, let me take an example from everyday life. Just as no one can set aside or add to a human covenant that has been duly established, so it is in this case.

GALATIANS 3:15

Hello Again, Lord ...

Thank you, Lord, for your promises and for the confidence that I can have in them.

What Was That Name Again?

Most of us know all too well the name of that person who tried his or her best to discourage us, that one girl or boy, man or woman who kept reminding us of our faults, that Coach of Negativity who stood on the sidelines of our race, shouting, "You can't do it. Who do you think you are anyway?"

We were doing just fine until he or she showed up, weren't we?

Maybe that person was someone we had previously considered a friend. Perhaps it was a family member. It might even have been someone we didn't know that well at all, but whose jealousy, insecurity, or just plain mean-spiritedness almost made us lose our focus and give in to self-doubt and fear.

It's hard to forget people like that, isn't it? We figure that people will be happy for us when we succeed. These kind of people aren't. We figure that no one would want to see us fail. These kind of people do. We figure that with all the discouragement that's in the world already, no one would want to create more. These type of people seem to enjoy every discouraging remark they make.

God knew that there would be discouragers in our lives. That's why he sends encouragers our way to help balance them out. If you're like most people, you know very well the name of that person who has always tried his or her best to encourage you. That girl or boy, man or woman who reminds you of your worth whenever you forget it. That person who overlooks your faults and sees your potential. That person who stands on the sidelines of your race, shouting, "Don't give up. You can do this! Don't you know who you are?"

Maybe that person is a friend, a family member, or even a total stranger. He or she may not even know how much his or her words of encouragement have positively affected your life. Yet no matter where you go in life, you'll never forget those words, you'll never forget their impact, and if you know it, you'll no doubt never forget that person's name.

Thoughts to Ponder

Who is the one person who has had the most positive impact on your life?

Have you told that person how much he or she has meant to you?

Bumper Sticker for the Day
Encouragement—fuel for life.

Scripture to Stand On

James, Peter, and John, those reputed to be pillars, gave me and Barnabas the right hand of fellowship when they recognized the grace given to me.

GALATIANS 2:9

Hello Again, Lord ...

Thank you, Lord, for the encouragers that you have sent into my life.

For Goodness Sake

D o you know anybody who's just plain good? Not good on the basketball court, although there are athletes who can make some pretty impressive baskets. Not good on a skateboard, or in the movies, or on a game show. I mean someone who's just a good person. Good in how he or she treats other people. Good in the things he or she does. Just plain good.

Do you know anyone like that?

We all do. And it's a good thing. Can you imagine what this world would be like without good people?

"You dropped your books. Ha! What a loser!"

"How come you're eating lunch all by yourself? If you don't have any friends, you should just skip lunch. You're making the rest of us feel uncomfortable."

"You're in trouble again? Hey, you asked for it. Don't expect any consolation from me."

That doesn't sound like a very good world to me. Thankfully, good people balance things out. Someone might laugh at you because you've dropped your books in the rush of trying to get to class on time, but then along comes someone else who offers to help. You might be sitting all alone in the cafeteria, but then someone sits down across from you and starts a conversation. And when things go wrong in your life, you might have to deal with heartless and uncaring people, but God also has a way of sending good people along at just the right time.

Thoughts to Ponder

Who in your life would you classify as a "good person"?

Have you told that person how much you appreciate them?

Bumper Sticker for the Day
Is "doing good" on your day planner?

Scripture to Stand On

But the fruit of the Spirit is ... goodness.

GALATIANS 5:22

Hello Again, Lord ...

Thank you, Lord, for all the good people you've sent into my life.

I Can't

I can't know everything, but I know God is faithful.

I can't see the future, but I know God is in charge of it.

I can't be everywhere, but I can be somewhere ... and make a difference.

I can't change anyone else, but I can change my attitude and outlook.

I can't have all the answers, but I know The Answer, and that's enough.

I can't solve the world's problems, but I can be part of a solution.

I can't change history, but something I do might change someone's future.

I can't give all the encouragement that someone might need, but I can give some of it.

I can't carry everyone's problems for them, but I can carry a few.

I can't be aware of every need, but I can be aware of one and do my best to meet it.

I can't hear every cry, but I can hear one cry and try to calm it.

I can't go everywhere, but I can go to one place and help.

I can't rewrite yesterday, but I can make sure tomorrow is better.

Thoughts to Ponder

List some of the things you can do to change your world.

Why do you think it's not the size of what you do that's important, but the fact that you do something?

Bumper Sticker for the Day
Do a little—change a lot.

Scripture to Stand On

I have been crucified with Christ and I no longer live, but Christ lives in me. The life I live in the body, I live by faith in the Son of god, who loved me and gave himself for me.

GALATIANS 2:20

Hello Again, Lord ...

Lord, help me not to second-guess what you can do through a willing vessel.

Adaptations

Have you ever adapted your behavior to fit in with a certain crowd? Have you ever found yourself not doing or saying certain things that you normally would do or say just because someone else was around and you were afraid of what he or she might think?

Here Paul points out the hypocrisy that he encountered among certain believers who were changing their usual behavior to accommodate the legalistic attitudes of those around them. Paul wanted them to be consistent. If the gospel is truly about grace, which it is, then Paul wanted them to be honest about that. He felt that when they said one thing and did another, they were acting hypocritically.

Do you find yourself holding others to standards to which you don't hold yourself?

Know what you believe and grant others the same grace and forgiveness you want for yourself. Be the same person with whomever you happen to be. Don't change convictions.

Thoughts to Ponder

Why do you think consistency is important to God?

Why is God's consistency important to you?

Bumper Sticker for the Day
Faith shouldn't be easily removable.

Scripture to Stand On

Before certain men came from James, he used to eat with the Gentiles. But when they arrived, he began to draw back and separate himself from the Gentiles.

GALATIANS 2:12a

Hello Again, Lord ...

Lord, help me not to play to my audience, but to be consistent with my faith.

Giveaways

Have you ever given away something, then as soon as it was gone, wanted it back, but by then it was too late?

"Here, take my ticket to the concert. It's OK, really. It's sold out and I know how much you want to go."

All that week, though, that's all you can think about. As Friday night rolls around and the hands on the clock start circling their way toward the eight o'clock hour, your regrets grow by the minute.

"I know my friend wanted to go to the concert, but I really wanted to go, too," you tell yourself. "Why'd I go and give away my ticket?"

It's good to be generous, but what if you later found out that this person didn't even go to the concert? He or she found something else to do that night instead? Your sacrifice wouldn't feel so good then, would it?

Do you know that there are some areas in life where we need to have clear boundaries? And they're a lot more valuable than concert tickets. For your emotional, physical, and spiritual health, you should have well-defined boundaries in many areas of your life. Know when to say no to situations or substances that could ultimately hurt you. Value yourself. Give away all the concert tickets that you want, but don't give away something that's irreplaceable—you.

Thoughts to Ponder

Why do you think it's important to stay true to your boundaries and to God's Word?

Are you comfortable with the lines that you've drawn in your relationships?

Bumper Sticker for the Day
Saying "no" to one thing can mean saying "yes" to
so much more.

Scripture to Stand On

The acts of the sinful nature are obvious: sexual immorality.

GALATIANS 5:19

Hello Again, Lord ...

Lord, help me to love myself enough to have healthy boundaries.

When I Was Meets I Am

Ever wish you could run away from your past? But you can't. It's always there, constantly reminding you that you're fallible. If only someone would give you a second chance, this time you'd do things right. You know you would. You wouldn't do this, you wouldn't do that, and you wouldn't even dream of doing that other thing. Yet people don't get second chances, do they?

They do when God steps on the scene. When I Am shows up, you become a whole new you.

When I Was meets I Am, the past is erased.
When I Was meets I Am, no stones are thrown.
When I Was meets I Am, worth is recognized.
When I Was meets I Am, the debt is forgiven.
When I Was meets I Am, hope is renewed.
When I Was meets I Am, love is evident.
When I Was meets I Am, peace is given.
When I Was meets I Am, joy is restored.
When I Was meets I Am, acceptance is felt.
When I Was meets I Am, guilt is released.
When I Was meets I Am, freedom is declared.
When I Was meets I Am, a new person is born.
When I Was meets I Am, the future is secured.
When I Was meets I Am, the amazing happens.

Thoughts to Ponder

How does it feel to know that with God you can become a brand-new person?

If God forgets your past wrongs, what good does it do for you to remember them?

Bumper Sticker for the Day
When God erases, there are no traces.

Scripture to Stand On

Neither circumcision nor uncircumcision means anything; what counts is a new creation.

GALATIANS 6:15

Hello Again, Lord ...

Lord, I thank you for making me a brand-new person.

In the Know

What do you know? What do you know beyond any doubt? What can no one talk you out of? What do you know that you know that you know that you know?

You know your name. You know which school you attend. You know the color of your eyes. There are certain things that you just know, aren't there? No one can come up to you and say you're somebody else. You'd know he or she was wrong and you were right. You wouldn't have to prove it to anyone. You'd just know it. No one could convince you that you don't go to the school that you go to, or that you have brown eyes instead of blue, or vice versa. You just know these things.

When you open a bank account, or if you ever apply for a credit card (hopefully not for many, many years), the application will most likely ask you a personal question for security purposes. It'll be something that you would know about yourself, but a stranger wouldn't. That's how the bank will know you're you, because you will be the only one who is able to answer their question correctly.

It's important to know the things that we know about ourselves and our lives. It's also important to know what we know about our faith, and to be unwavering in it.

Know about God. Read his Word, develop a relationship with him, and find our as much as you can about his character. Know that you know that you know that you know it. Know it so well that no one can talk you out of it. When it comes to your faith, be in the know.

Thoughts to Ponder

What do you know about your faith in God?

Why do you think it's important to be unwavering when it comes to your faith?

Bumper Sticker for the Day
Ye shall know the truth, and never let go of it.

Scripture to Stand On

You foolish Galatians! Who has bewitched you? Before your very eyes Jesus Christ was clearly portrayed as crucified.

GALATIANS 3:1

Hello Again, Lord ...

Lord, help me to stay true to the truth of your gospel.

Law and God's Order

It's all a matter of attitude ...

Pharisees	**Jesus**
This women was caught in the very act of adultery.	He who is without sin, cast the first stone.
How many times is that guy going to fail?	Forgive seventy times seven.
Why doesn't she act more like a Christian?	First take the plank out of your own eye, then you'll see clearly to remove the speck from your brother's eye.
I'm glad I don't act like that!	For all have sinned and come short of the glory of God.
My goodness is enough.	No one is good, except God alone.
What would God do without me?	The first will be last and the last will be first.

Pharisees	**Jesus**
"We don't like his kind."	There will be more rejoicing in heaven over one sinner who repents than over ninety-nine righteous persons.
Why are you associating with someone like that?	It is not the healthy who need a doctor, but the sick.
He'll never change.	With God, all things are possible.
God is going to judge you someday. But until he does, I'm filling in for him.	Forgive us our trespasses as we forgive those who trespass against us.
But he ...	Love each other.
But she ...	Love each other.
You need to do more.	I am the Way, the Truth, and the Life.
You are condemned by the law.	I lay down my life for the sheep.
And another thing ...	It is finished.

Thoughts to Ponder

Have you ever encountered a Pharisee?

What is your definition of grace?

Bumper Sticker for the Day
If we could do it on our own, Calvary would have been cancelled.

Scripture to Stand On

I do not set aside the grace of God, for if righteousness could be gained through the law, Christ died for nothing!

GALATIANS 2:21

Hello Again, Lord ...

Lord, protect me against Pharisees, and help me to not be one to others.